JOSEPH W. DANIELS JR.
CHRISTIE LATONA

CONNECTING FOR A CHANGE

How to Engage People, Churches, and Partners to Inspire Hope in Your Community

Nashville

CONNECTING FOR A CHANGE:
HOW TO ENGAGE PEOPLE, CHURCHES, AND PARTNERS TO INSPIRE HOPE IN YOUR COMMUNITY

Copyright ©2019 by Abingdon Press

All rights reserved.

No part of this work may be reproduced or transmitted in any form or by any means, electronic or mechanical, including photocopying and recording, or by any information storage or retrieval system, except as may be expressly permitted by the 1976 Copyright Act or in writing from the publisher. Requests for permission should be addressed to Permissions, Abingdon Press, 2222 Rosa L. Parks Boulevard, Nashville, TN 37228-1306, or permissions@abingdonpress.com.

This book is printed on acid-free paper.

Library of Congress Cataloging-in-Publication Data has been requested.

ISBN 978-1-5018-7437-6

Scripture unless otherwise noted is from the Common English Bible. Copyright © 2011 by the Common English Bible. All rights reserved. Used by permission. www.CommonEnglishBible.com.

Scripture quotations marked MSG are taken from THE MESSAGE, copyright © 1993, 1994, 1995, 1996, 2000, 2001, 2002 by Eugene H. Peterson. Used by permission of NavPress. All rights reserved. Represented by Tyndale House Publishers, Inc.

19 20 21 22 23 24 25 26 27 28—10 9 8 7 6 5 4 3 2 1
MANUFACTURED IN THE UNITED STATES OF AMERICA

More Praise for *Connecting for a Change*

"I have witnessed the authentic power of connection at work through the lives of my friends Christy and Joe for many years. I have also observed them in the building of lasting relationships, the organizing of people for change, the effective utilization of assets, and the liberating of congregations across our country. This book is going to create bridges of hope across the historical expanse of division and distrust for churches and the people who lead and serve."
—**Rudy Rasmus**, author of *Touch, Jesus Insurgency,* and *Love Period*

"Joe and Christie know mission strategy. They live it, dream it, and teach it. They will flip some of your expectations upside down as they seek to teach and model for us how to build relationships, organize people, utilize our assets, and liberate our congregations."
—**Duane Anders**, senior pastor, Cathedral of the Rockies (UMC), Boise, ID

"*Connecting for a Change* will help you understand that relational health is the biblical foundation of all ministry. Daniels and Latona identify the critical pitfalls to avoid. They show how trust is built. They encourage and help congregations experience the joy of vital ministry that transforms lives inside the church and in the communities we serve."
—**Tom Berlin**, lead pastor, Floris UMC, Herndon, VA

"Daniels and Latona demonstrate the breakdown that occurs in our communities when we fail to take the time to connect with each other. The writers share transparent and personal stories, refuting our excuses, releasing us from complacency, and counteracting our rationalizations. They challenge and equip us to reach out to others, to actively engage, and to embrace change."
—**Olu Brown**, senior pastor, Impact Church (UMC), Atlanta, GA

"This book is for those who share the authors' passion for connecting people, churches, and partners to inspire hope and life change in their communities. With rich biblical examples, the authors develop four building blocks for vitality that turn distrust and division into courage and competence to help communities thrive."
—**Lovett H. Weems Jr**, distinguished professor of church leadership, Wesley Theological Seminary, Washington, DC

Other Abingdon Press Books by Joseph W. Daniels Jr.

*Walking with Nehemiah: Your Community Is
Your Congregation*

Contents

Acknowledgments — vii

Foreword by Olivia Gross — xi

Introduction — xiii

CHAPTER 1:
Build Relationships — 1

CHAPTER 2:
Organize People — 15

CHAPTER 3:
Utilize Assets — 33

CHAPTER 4:
Liberate Congregations — 51

CHAPTER 5:
Inspire Hope — 71

APPENDIX:
Tips for Judicatory Leaders — 79

Notes — 97

For additional resources, visit www.connectingforachange.org.

Acknowledgments

Whenever writing about one's story, or whenever sharing beliefs about what is possible or how things could be done better, it is natural for some readers to read things into the text that simply are not there. We want to lift up the fact that we are sharing out of our rich experience that includes so many people who have shaped, taught, shared, laughed, and cried with us. We are not writing this as solo experts as much as witnesses to what we discovered feeds mission innovation and what starves it. There are so many people to acknowledge for this book—so many that it would take more space than we have available to write. But there are some specific acknowledgements that need to be made.

First, we thank our bishops in this process—Bishop Marcus Matthews, who was the episcopal leader during our work together on the Greater Washington District of the Baltimore–Washington Conference of The United Methodist Church, and Bishop Latrelle Miller Easterling, who is the current episcopal leader of the Baltimore–Washington Conference. Without Bishop Matthews's vision and openness to see the possibilities of dual leadership, and attempts at creative and innovative leadership, this book would not have come to pass. And, without Bishop Easterling's support, encouragement, and extension of bold, collaborative, courageous leadership, we wouldn't be here as well. Thanks to both of you for your tremendous leadership; we've been blessed to have two very fine episcopal leaders to lead our church!

Acknowledgments

Second, we acknowledge the phenomenal people of the Greater Washington District, with a special shout out to our district administrator, Olivia Gross, and our connecting elders (some of whom only served one year): Miguel Balderas, Jalene Chase-Sands, Johnsie Cogman, Rachel Cornwell, Gerald Elston, Ron Foster, David Hall, Brian Jackson, Cary James, Paul Johnson, Fay Lundin, Martha Meredith, Ianther Mills, Charlie Parker, Adam Snell, Ron Triplett, and Stacey Cole Wilson. Without the dedication and leadership of these leaders, the vision of "Claim Your ZIP Codes for Christ," and the enthusiasm it generated, the initiative would not have caught fire! Blessings to each one of you!

Third, we thank Dr. Duane Anders, lead pastor at Boise First United Methodist Church in Boise, Idaho (The Cathedral of the Rockies) in the Oregon/Idaho Annual Conference, and the wonderful leaders of the California-Nevada Annual Conference. I (Joe) was not the first dual appointment as DS/pastor in our denomination. And I (Christie) wasn't the first resource person deployed at a regional level. We weren't the first persons to attempt this work, but like all pioneers, experienced the joys and trials inherent in forging fresh paths.

When the opportunity was granted by Bishop Matthews for me to do the dual role, I (Joe) immediately contacted one of my dear friends and colleagues, Duane Anders. I had pondered about DS's being pastors at the same time for some thirteen years; Duane had actually done it. And while Duane was not the first dual appointment (DS/pastor) in our connection, he held the longest tenure that I knew of, and was the newest to this style of leadership within our denomination. We had developed a very long, deep relationship in a national clergy incubator group that has been almost fifteen years running. Duane's insight into strategy, self-care, and staff support for this journey was overwhelmingly helpful as we sought to get our bearings on this new task before us. Duane, we both say, thank you!

One of the projects that I (Christie) was working on at the beginning of this new work was with the California-Nevada Annual Conference, who had undergone a strategic planning and restructuring that entailed dividing

Acknowledgments

each massive district into smaller circuits. My job was to help them assess the degree to which things were working and areas of needed improvement. This afforded us the opportunity to learn (and affirm) lessons that consultation had revealed and create helpful dialogue partnerships with persons from across the connection—from United Methodist leaders to circuit leaders to district superintendents to the director of Connectional Ministries and beyond. Thank you for allowing a 360 degree look on a conference-wide model!

Fourth, a huge thank you to the people of the Emory United Methodist Church in Washington, DC, otherwise known as The Emory Fellowship. You made a monumental sacrifice, sharing your pastor with a district of sixty six churches, and this was by no means an easy task, particularly with an emerging multi-million dollar building project. There were successes and failures along the way, but thanks be to God, we grew through it and have been the better for it! To God be the glory!

Last, but not least, we thank our families. We are both family-oriented people, with wonderful family support, and Lord knows, without family, ministry is simply not possible for either of us. To the Daniels family—Madelyn, Joia, Joey, and Tiffany—and the Latona family—Peter, Melina, Andrew, and Christopher—we want you to know how grateful we are to be a part of you and how much you inspire us!

Foreword

When people cross our path, we are hardly ever conscious of the impact they will have on our life's journey. Some leave an indelible mark and change the trajectory of where we thought our life was heading.

Prior to serving as administrator for the Greater Washington District, I knew of Joe Daniels and Christie Latona. But knowing something about a person and actually knowing that person is like knowing the sounds of a language and knowing how to speak that language.

The language I learned to speak as I became the third part of the triad that served the Greater Washington District was mission strategy. My involvement with the district team moved me from knowing about mission strategy to being actively involved in the details and hard work of what it means to be in mission with God's people and the community that God entrusts to our care.

The beauty and challenge of that relationship was that Joe and Christie led by example. The work was intense, collaborative, frustrating at times, yet fulfilling. Days were long, calendars were full, and barriers were present. Nevertheless, they were committed to their call to change mind-sets and hearts, while proclaiming the message of what it means to be missionally engaged with God's people.

The process of prayer and discernment led to the strategy of organizing churches by zip codes to multiply their effectiveness and maximize their potential. The district's missional campaign was focused on how to engage each congregation to "claim their zip codes for Jesus Christ," not as lone rangers, but in collaboration with other congregations in those zip codes. The result was a joining of congregations (within those zip codes) of different sizes, cultures, abilities, resources, and energies, organized into clusters with a cluster leader, collaborating as one to make changes in their surrounding communities. The major change was to cluster the churches by proximity rather than by affinity.

Joe's message to the churches was a reminder that Jesus met people where they were, but did not leave them as he found them. Jesus always filled a tangible need while offering people salvation. As Jesus's hands and feet in the world, we were to do the same. That task could not be accomplished if we did not step outside of our walls. The church could no longer afford to function in total disregard of the surrounding community.

Joe's message to the congregations at the first cluster church conference was the story of Philip and the Ethiopian eunuch (Acts 8:26-40). The portion of that message that most influenced my work (our work) was when Philip asked the eunuch, "Do you really understand what you are reading?" He said, "Without someone to guide me, how could I?" This was the main principle of all we did: guiding each cluster to look outside of themselves, to see what was around them, where the church needed to step in to fill a tangible need.

This experience changed my perspective of the meaning of mission strategy. It is a language I learned to speak and understand fluently because of the work and dedication of two people who had a vision for what we are capable of doing if we are willing to do the work, stay the course, and believe what Jesus meant when he said, "Go and do likewise" (Luke 10:37).

—Olivia Gross
Greater Washington District Administrator,
Baltimore–Washington Conference; Pastor, Mount Zion
United Methodist Church, Olney, MD

Introduction

Just as God brings order out of chaos in the book of Genesis, God causes connection to take place in spaces and places where a history of disconnection once prevailed. God will bring people from different races, cultures, ethnicities, classes, and the like to infuse connection in ways that work to unite previously divided people and communities together for positive change and the common good. God will open opportunities for us to engage people, churches, and partners to inspire hope in communities in ways we'd never imagine.

Neither of us would ever have thought that an African American male pastor (Joe) of a predominantly black, multicultural church in the District of Columbia would have connected with a white female church and private sector strategic consultant (Christie) based in the Maryland suburbs to pursue a common mission of advancing God's reign in local, regional, national, and international ways. But after an unexpected encounter during which Christie's work brought her to Joe's congregation, missional connection happened and a desire to develop and expand mission strategy emerged. And as God would have it, when Joe became the district superintendent (DS) of the Greater Washington District while continuing to pastor Emory (where Christie had become a member), we came to understand deeply the need to teach leaders—laity and clergy—about the importance of focusing on the mission and having a strategy for doing so. Jesus's mission and the mission of his church is to liberate souls, systems, and societies so that people can live life and live it to the fullest. This requires a liberated church that loves beyond the barriers and that demonstrates in words and deeds that unconditional love can get us to the places and spaces where we must be, have to be, and will be.

As we look at the lives of Jesus, Nehemiah, and Moses and at our own experience, mission strategy is this: a divinely inspired plan to build relationships, organize people, utilize assets, and liberate congregations for the thriving of communities. To do mission strategy, one has to believe that with God all things are possible and has to see those possibilities as vibrantly as one sees the difficulties. To do mission strategy, one has to come to the task with the intention to discern God's will and purpose, not for self-aggrandizement.

The change we sought to bring to the mission field, when we teamed up as DS and strategist, was to connect people, churches, and partners to inspire hope and life change in their communities. We saw the possibility for the church to change its perspective and we saw the opportunity to change the community's view of the church. There were churches that were dying and we saw the opportunity to bring life through turnaround strategies, through an infusion of hope through worship, discipleship, and community engagement. There were churches that had literally ignored or turned their backs on the communities around them and were wondering why they were declining. Their hope was right under their nose. We found that connecting for a change was sorely needed.

When we started talking with leaders in the church, we found:

- Disconnection between clergy and clergy, laity and laity, clergy and laity, between churches and their communities, between clergy, laity, their churches, and/or their governing body.

- Division along lines of race, class, ethnicity, theology, gender, geography, and congregation sizes.

- Distrust of one another (clergy of laity, laity of laity, clergy of clergy) and to the body or bodies to which they relate.

- Disbelief in the value and power of connection.

Introduction

These are the thieves coming to steal, kill, and destroy, as Jesus speaks of in John 10. These are the enemies of mission strategy. All mission strategy should have at its core both being and offering Christ to the world—"I came so that they could have life—indeed, so that they could live life to the fullest" (John 10:10)—with systems put in place that create an ecosystem that keeps healthy connection at the forefront. Unfortunately, both the church and society seek to create exclusive ecosystems, that is, environments for some groups of people at the exclusion of others. When there are incomplete, unjust, or imbalanced ecosystems, chaos and confusion are ushered in. Anger and hatred grow and are provoked. These ecosystems create pathways for people's demise, destruction, and decay, not only for congregations, but for communities of people as well. One only needs to reflect on the current opioid crisis that is gutting rural and suburban communities left and right. Or to reflect on the proliferation of the prison industrial complex that is the largest of any nation in the world and doesn't actually help people become whole. Or the never-ending political battles, rhetoric, and vilification of people that allow an unjust, incomplete immigration policy to exist.

The task of mission strategy is to connect for a change.

Building relationships, organizing people, utilizing assets, and liberating congregations are the multipliers of mission strategy. Disconnection, division, distrust, and disbelief are the enemies of mission strategy. The challenge for anyone engaged in mission strategy is to stay focused on the multipliers while wary of the enemies. We must know what the enemies are and where they are located in our contexts, and we must intentionally focus our energy and attention on the multipliers.

When unchecked or fed, these enemies create a very toxic environment. In our context, this toxicity can infiltrate churches, districts, annual conferences, and infect the connection as a whole. The problem that our church faces today is that it has too often succumbed to the enemy and has thus gotten used to operating in a toxic environment. Some would say, it's the "new" normal. However, healthy mission strategy actively drives out toxins through injecting and focusing on the multipliers—building relationships, organizing people, utilizing assets, and liberating congregations—for people to experience an alternative reality: life-giving connections.

A Developmental Approach

Connecting for a Change is written for a wide variety of leaders in a wide variety of contexts with the belief that anyone can learn mission strategy. It is our prayer that this book helps bishops, superintendents, judicatory leaders, clergy, laity, and congregations learn how to develop vibrant ecosystems that support all people having life and living it to the full.

When we work with people on developing proficiency with the four basic multipliers of mission strategy—building relationships, organizing people, utilizing assets, and liberating congregations—we find that most people are good in at least one area, but are unaware of the need for all other multipliers. For example, some people come to the task of mission strategy great at building relationships, but struggling with utilizing assets. Or others are great organizers of people, but are in need of liberation. Below is a developmental continuum that describes the stages of growth for each multiplier. In the first four chapters, the nature of the dimension has been articulated within a biblical framework, and then each of the three stages along the developmental continuum is unpacked. We recommend that readers read through the book in its entirety, go to www.connectingforachange.org to download assessments and exercises, and use the results to focus on the section of a chapter that pertains to their particular stage in development.

Introduction

Developmental Continuum

There is no shame in being a beginner. As astrophysicist Neil deGrasse Tyson stated: it is "curious that we spend more time congratulating people who have succeeded than encouraging people who have not."[1] We encourage readers to identify where they are along the continuum and to take their next faithful step to successful mission strategy.

Chapter 1
Build Relationships

Ministry without relationships is like a car without gas. Like a lamp without an outlet to plug into. Like a human without oxygen. Without relationships, life cannot exist. Without relationships, life cannot thrive. You can't even think of doing mission strategy without intentional relationship building. No relationships, no church. No relationships, a fractured community. No relationships, chaos. The church engaging in mission strategy often discovers a world filled with broken relationships needing to be rebuilt or relationships that have never begun because of divisions, misperceptions, busyness, or no effort. And so, the building of relationships among clergy, laity, the church, and community is an essential starting point. Where relationships are missing, God sends us to start them. Where relationships are possible, God commissions us to make them. Where relationships have begun, God inspires us to grow and develop them for a profound impact.

Stop Missing Relationships

Each person you encounter in a day is an opportunity to begin connecting. The centerpiece of Jesus's ministry was found in building relationships. Everywhere he went, he started new ones. He specialized in starting relationships with the very people with whom others didn't want to be bothered. Like the woman at the well who was shunned because of her shame. Like the man at the pool at Bethesda who had been there thirty-eight years and couldn't get beyond his stuck situation. And the list goes on. He also specialized in growing and nurturing relationships with family, disciples, and his companions.

Each person you encounter in a day is an opportunity to begin connecting.

Leaders must intentionally start new relationships and deepen existing relationships every opportunity they have. Not only is it the right thing to do, but also it is one of the essential ways in which we practice following and growing closer to Jesus. It is a spiritual discipline to see Jesus in the people we encounter and to love them as Jesus loves them. The server at the restaurant, the homeless person you pass each day, the family who comes to your food pantry, the person you sit next to on public transit, the shopkeeper, and even (especially) your neighbor are all examples of people you may not realize are potential new relationships. As our friend Bob Farr would say, "get their name" and learn their story.[1] In so doing, they are no longer simply our neighbors, our servers, or strangers; they are Hector, Jimmy, and Judy—people who are fully human, with faces, stories, and lives.

Without us knowing someone's story, our view of that person is formed by our own biases and first impressions. Not only is *beauty* in the eye of the beholder, but everything else is too. Reflect on those times when your judgment of someone has negatively impacted your ability to treat him or her as a child of God. You don't know what you don't know about other people. What about the parent screaming at her child at the store, making you uncomfortable and righteously indignant? She just received word that a loved one died. The neighbor who is exceedingly rude and thoughtless, irritating you every time you encounter him? He is struggling with depression. Challenge yourself to see beyond your first impression of people and to start seeking to actually know people.

Not only is *beauty* in the eye of the beholder, but everything else is too.

When Jesus was asked what was the greatest commandment, he didn't hesitate: love the Lord your God with all your heart, mind, soul, and strength and love your neighbor as yourself. The neighboring movement in the United States takes this idea literally and focuses on getting church members to neighbor well.[2] The starting point for this movement was to have church members learn the names of their neighbors and plan a block party. The fruit of these simple steps was tangible, as people stopped missing the opportunity to build relationships and started to transform lives and relationships. Start new relationships and deepen existing relationships every opportunity you have and watch Jesus work.

The low-hanging fruit in each congregation and community is seeing all the people in your midst and getting to know them. Powerful things happen when we are intentional about this![3] Our church's recent Good Friday community witness initiative provides a good example of this. For the last four years, our congregation has been engaged in a major housing, commercial, and congregational development project, and as a result we've been "nomadic"—having no central place to meet, worshipping in schools and synagogues. It's been critically important for us to be intentional about maintaining a presence with people in our church's community in Washington, DC. So, we have undertaken certain projects as a congregation to build relationships with the community. On Good Friday, we gave the congregation the assignment of visiting the laundromat in their communities and doing the following: (1) introduce ourselves to as many people as we could in the laundromat; (2) as conversations developed, offer the person we met $2.00 in coins to help with his or her laundry expenses; and (3) see if the Holy Spirit creates an opportunity to share.

Because it is important for the leaders to model what it is we want to see, I (Joe) went out with my wife to the laundromat down the street from our church. We spoke with African Americans, Latinos, East Indians, and Africans, and the encounters were rich. Of course, some people wanted to know who we were, some people didn't want to talk with us at all, others were suspicious, and still others were extremely grateful for our kindness. When we introduced ourselves and our church to one family, they immediately knew who I was. Turns out, the husband was a college classmate of one of our worship leaders, had visited the church years before, and had just returned to DC, with his family. They were without a church home and were looking. We started building the relationship with that conversation, and the Lord opened up the opportunity to invite the couple to church. Lo and behold, on Easter Sunday, during the passing of the peace at the first service, there they were, glad to be in the fellowship. And they've been worshipping with us ever since. Things happen when we are intentional about building relationships!

Let us be clear. The goal of relationship building is *not* getting people to come to your church. It is developing a relationship that God can take anywhere God wants to take it. Once, we were teaching about how to do one-on-one relational meeting at a conference and had someone volunteer to role-play with us. In spite of our directions, each time she opened her mouth she couldn't stop talking about why the person should come to her church. This is a turnoff for most people during an initial conversation. We must always get to know people first. Be obedient to the prompting of the Holy Ghost instead of your desperation.

> **The goal of relationship building is *not* getting people to come to your church. It is developing a relationship that God can take anywhere God wants to take it.**

If you want to change the system in which you operate, change the amount and quality of relationship building. As leaders we need to develop the practice of spending as much time as we can building relationships.

Usually this occurs on the street and in the communities where we serve and not in our offices. In our first week of work as superintendent and strategist for the sixty-six churches in our locale, we got out of our offices and went to visit a prominent pastor in our district. We'd never met him, had heard a lot of great things about him, and wanted to get to know him. When we sat down in his office, we let him know that we came with no agenda, that we just came to visit. Sometimes in this social media–crazed world, we need to just get to know people and listen to them. During the conversation, the pastor said, "Joe, you are my sixth superintendent in four years. I feel disconnected from the conference and from the rest of my colleagues on the district. If you can help build and rebuild these connections, you will have done well." We set out to do just that.

Even blind Bartimaeus—though he could not see Jesus coming, but could hear and feel his presence—yelled out for Jesus to start a new relationship: "Jesus, Son of David, show me mercy!" (Mark 10:47). When you read the story, you quickly discover that those around him implored him to stop trying to make connection. But Bartimaeus, seeking to make a connection for a change and knowing that if he missed out on this relationship, may never have a chance to see again, was persistent. And because he was persistent, he regained his sight—his vision for a brighter future.[4]

> *In a typical week, what keeps you from making real connection with others? What keeps you from connecting with people you don't know?*

So often we miss out on the blessings God has for us simply because we stop getting to know people. We do not pause to entertain the stranger unaware. More frequently than not, the blessing we need and the blessing we can be to someone else is just a shout away. When we stop missing relationship opportunities, we will start discovering that the God we serve is greater than we could ever imagine.

Chapter 1

Start Making Relationships

We miss out on connection when we view people as objects instead of as human beings created in God's image. When we look at the Gospels, we find Jesus having encounter after encounter with people whom others looked upon as less than human, but whom he treated with dignity and honored their value. One such story is our Lord's interaction with the woman caught in adultery. Others wanted to kill her for her transgression. If they had seen her as a human being created in God's image, they wouldn't have picked up any stones, but would have sought to understand her story and start the making of relationship right there. That's what Jesus did—he found her at her point of need and then began to connect with her. Too often we don't connect with others, but instead treat and view ourselves and our neighbors as problems to avoid or fix, and not as people to connect with and cherish. Too often we judge and condemn others rather than discover the blessing that they are to us and the world. Connecting for a change means we intentionally need to start making relationships.

The types of relationships we need to be making are authentic, not transactional. We have tons of experiences in and outside of the church in which people have sought to relate to us transactionally rather than authentically. From people seeking to win us over to their political agenda to people seeking to use us or our positions to get things done to transactions around race or gender. We could fill these pages with numerous examples of how people have sought to relate to us based on what we can provide them rather than on who we are as human beings made in the image of God with particular callings and visions. Perhaps you have experiences like those as well.

> **Too often we judge and condemn others rather than discover the blessing that they are to us and the world.**

Transactional relationships are built, essentially, on self-focused desires rather than on empathy, trust, or genuine care for others. Think about relationships you know of that are focused on greed, pride, and lust for power or pleasure. These are probably transactional relationships. *You have something I want or can help me get it. So, I will be in relationship with you in order to get what I want.* Transactional relationships are generally fragile, brittle, and a precarious balance of power, in which at least one person is committed only to personal gain of some kind, not to the other person or to the relationship itself. It is extremely difficult to influence another person or to bring change of any kind in a transactional relationship. In fact, transactional relationships are *not* really relationships, because in them people do not truly relate to one another; they relate only to their own need or desire. The result is the ultimate "frenemies"—people who call one another "friend," but who think and behave like enemies. Some denominations right now are seeing this play out vividly over the issues of racism and full inclusion of LGBTQI individuals. Authentic relationships are the best defense against the enemies of mission strategy—disconnection, distrust, division, and disbelief.

One of the ways that transactional interactions surface in local churches is in the area of evangelism. When we work with churches on revitalization, we regularly hear some refrains including: "We need to attract more [*insert predominant demographic in the community*] people so that they become members and help our church stay open." That blank is sometimes *young families, young people, Hispanic/Latinos,* and so on. The target isn't as important as the mistaken dynamic: engagement in vampire evangelism instead of relational evangelism. Churches have abundant life to offer people in our communities, but when churches shift their focus to maintenance instead of mission and to survival instead of saving souls, the gospel reality is forgotten. The church that sees its mission field primarily as a means of keeping itself alive will not be successful in making relationships. Churches succeed in making relationships when they wholeheartedly view their mission field as an opportunity to share God's love in relevant, enthusiastic, and authentic ways.

Chapter 1

One of the churches in our district found itself in a community that had transitioned from 10 percent to 80 percent Hispanic/Latino over the course of eight years. One of its most active leaders almost single-handedly started and maintained a food pantry that was well attended by the community. However, when the people from the community came to the pantry, to worship, or to any other church activity, they struggled to find hospitality from this individual and others in the congregation who were seeking to have the Hispanic/Latino community "behave" as new members were expected to. We worked with this leader, aiming to help her discover a better way of engaging with people who were from socio-economic backgrounds and ethnic groups other than her own. She protested: "After everything we have done for them, they haven't volunteered to help with the ministry, they haven't joined the church, and they haven't tithed." Her heart and efforts were so focused on keeping her church alive as it had been that she couldn't see how she was missing the opportunity to actually build relationships. People were treated as objects, not human beings. The food pantry was an honest effort to be relevant and provided a chance for the church to be the hands and feet of Christ. However, the way in which this was done (*to and for* people instead of *with* them) and why it was done (to get people to join the church) made it ultimately counterproductive. Because this woman (and others) did not welcome people with enthusiasm and authentic love, nor treat them with respect, the people did not sense that they were really welcome as part of the church, and so they did not meaningfully participate. Instead of offering help and hope to people in the community, the church gained a reputation for being unfriendly and unwelcoming of its neighbors. Unconditional love calls us to a much higher place than this. Unconditional love calls for building relationships with the very people whom God has placed in our midst. Not for our sake, but to connect for a change, for the sake of the kingdom.

One of the things that surprised us as we sought to build collaborative teams of church leaders for greater impact is the degree to which unhealthy competition can get in the way. Competition like this can prevent us from building relationships with the very people God may have sent us to extend or strengthen ministry. We wish that every leader understood that they are not competing against others, but instead competing for loving God and neighbor better. In fact, we believe one of the markers of spiritual maturity is found in the quality and quantity of relationships for the sake of God's reign. From local churches to clusters of churches, there are examples of how we get it wrong and how we get it right.

One of our churches was seeking to integrate and improve their sound and multimedia ministry. They discovered someone with expertise in sound ministry and asked her to lead. She created a plan and started to implement it—including adding new equipment and wiring—without having invested in building relationships with the old leaders of the ministry who felt they had ownership of the sound and, up until that point, had the most knowledge in the congregation. One of the existing leaders was offended that she was not consulted or named lead of the new multimedia ministry, which led to her firing off several e-mails to the congregational leader responsible for this decision. After many conversations, forgiveness was extended between these two people because they developed a relationship through the course of their conversations, even though the circumstances were unpleasant. However, no relationship was forged between the old and new leaders of the multimedia ministry. So, the unhealthy competitive spirit prevailed, weakening the impact of the ministry. It is a picture of the difficulties that can take place within a church body when we ignore the importance of making relationships.

Unfortunately, this scenario plays out amongst clergy, too. When we did the initial gathering of twenty-plus leaders to discern what a DC-based young adult planting zone might look like, one leader dropped out immediately because she wanted to do something at her church and didn't see value in collaborating across congregations. As the core leadership team emerged for this effort, we had to wrestle with "who gets to count" new people who get engaged in this new faith expression. We had to answer the question in a way that didn't double-count persons and that created a "win-win" or "both-and" so that partnering was maintained. We learned that, in general, we are much better at partnering in service projects than at planting new faith expressions. We were beginning to toy with the idea of reimagining reporting to include numbers for the cluster of churches so that all churches would begin to focus more on the mission field rather than on their individual church statistics. Sometimes churches won't even build relationships with other churches in their communities because they see those churches as "the competition" rather than being on the same team.

Transformative connections happen when we build authentic relationships, not transactional ones!

Don't make excuses for why leaders and congregations aren't in relationship. Start making relationships even with people who haven't been engaged and even with people who put up initial resistance. One vital leader in our district was full of excuses when we went to him to build relationship. "The best thing you can do for me," he told us, "is to leave me alone. If you just let me do what I've been sent here to do, then everything will be alright." *Whoa!* we thought. But after listening to him for another thirty minutes, we discovered that he'd not had great relationships with superintendents and denominational staff. Not because he was not a great person; he was. And not because the superintendents and conference staff were bad people; they were good people, too. However, the reality for him up to that point was, whenever he'd been approached in the past about serving in the annual conference, he was always asked to serve on a committee or a board that had nothing to do with his primary focus and passion in ministry—prayer, ministry with the poor, and making disciples. And so when we shared with him that we did not want him to serve on a committee, but wanted him to help shape ministry with other pastors and congregations in his mission field, he got excited! He ended up becoming a "connecting elder," one of the leaders we selected in the spirit of Exodus 18 to convene a group of pastors and congregations to impact their mission field in a greater fashion. Resolving hunger became their focus, and suddenly this pastor, who wanted to have nothing to do with anything resembling the annual conference, became a champion for mission strategy in his community and a key leader for connecting pastors and congregations passionately in ministry. His cluster even spearheaded a twenty-plus-mile prayer walk around his cluster's mission field as an attempt to meet people on the street, foster new connections, and build new relationships between congregations that had been disconnected "competitors." Transformative connections happen when we build authentic relationships, not transactional ones!

How might you or your congregation be treating people as commodities instead of human beings with unique stories?

Keep Molding Relationships

With Jesus at the center of our relationships, our connections lead us toward our full potential and the possibility for transformed lives. When Jesus sat in the middle of Peter's boat and told him to put out into the deep and let down his nets for a catch after a long night of catching nothing, Peter found himself in the middle of a great transformation and blessing for him and those around. They caught more fish than they could possibly imagine, so much that they had to call for a second boat to bring in this economic boom. But more than that, they were transformed from fishers of fish to fishers of people. Their call and purpose was revealed, and from that point, their lives and the lives of countless others were never the same. Who else but Jesus would come up to a failed fisherman and invite him to be his running buddy and right-hand man on the journey to save souls? Mission strategy requires us to see what is not yet present, and not get distracted by evidence of death and failure, so that we can strive toward God's preferred future.

Chapter 1

When you allow Jesus to be Lord of your relationships, greater things will happen. There was a new member at a church in our district who had a passion for reaching people who usually wouldn't dare think of going to church. She had recently been delivered from a life of substance abuse and from a profession requiring few clothes. She was filled with new ideas for creating environments for people who usually wouldn't come to a church. The church was already deeply involved in building relationships with unhoused neighbors, but the woman wanted the church to do more to integrate an even wider cross-section of the community. The tricky part was that she didn't trust most people and was driving leaders inside the church crazy. She didn't do things the "right" way, and her tenacity and tone weren't what the leaders were used to. Those in leadership were driving her crazy when they tried to support her in complying with the church's best practices and procedures. It wasn't unusual for her to get upset and curse someone out—in an e-mail or in person. She often felt that she wasn't being treated with the same respect as other ministry leaders, and her way of dealing with that was lashing out. It would have been really easy to have just stopped interacting, and some leaders tried to do so. Except, that's not what Jesus would have done.

Mission strategy requires us to see what is not yet present, and not get distracted by evidence of death and failure, so that we can strive toward God's preferred future.

Often our interactions with "difficult" people give us the opportunity to go deeper in our own discipleship by allowing Jesus to be Lord and to guide us in our interactions. When we allow Jesus to be Lord, we see the good and the God in others. When we allow Jesus to be Lord, we experience the peace in operating from our God-self instead of our ego-self. When we allow Jesus to be Lord, we shift from being right to being love. When we allow Jesus to be Lord, we let go of the notion that ministry is all up to us and simply follow. When we allow Jesus to be Lord, we stop praying for God to change others or to change the situation and start praying for God to change us, for us to learn. When leaders allow Jesus to be Lord of this relationship, they become aware of the living Christ in new ways, and engaging in even difficult relationships becomes a spiritual practice.

The "difficult" woman moved out of state a couple of years after she joined the church. Recently she was back in town to help the church celebrate a momentous occasion. She started crying when she saw many of the members and apologized profusely for how she had treated them. Many honestly thanked her for helping them deepen their own discipleship and told her she had been forgiven years ago.

It is all about relationship. Many people feel that the first disciples were just called by Jesus and they got up and followed him. The truth of the matter is that Jesus spent time at the fishing dock—"sitting on the dock of the bay watching the tide roll away," as Otis Redding sang it years ago—building relationships with the fishermen he would one day call. The truth of the matter is that Jesus spent many hours at banquets, interacting with the haves and have-nots, people who accepted him and those who rejected him, seeking to find and build relationships that would transform the world. The truth of the matter is that Jesus hung out at weddings, turning water into wine, so that parties could continue, people could get to know each other much more deeply, and ministry could begin to happen. Jesus is our model for relationship building. Jesus is our model for connecting for a change. Start building relationships!

Where are you and your church molding and being molded by the relationships you are building?

Chapter 2
Organize People

Ministry without organizing people is like a car with a disassembled engine. Like a lamp without a power cord. Like a human who is disconnected from meaningful community. If we don't organize people, organizations get stuck and become introverted. Without organized people, the church is impotent. Even if you are building relationships, utilizing assets, and liberating congregations, you cannot implement mission strategy without organizing people to transform lives and create holistic community for the common good. And so, organizing clergy, laity, the church, and community to connect for a change is critical to leading people to have life and live it to the full. Where we are complacent in organizing people, God often challenges us to go deeper with God and neighbor. Where organizing people is half-hearted, God disturbs us to be committed. Where we are consistently organizing people, God empowers courageous souls to cross lines of division and to plant and water seeds of revival that make tangible, holistic differences in one another's lives.

Shake off Complacency

In many parts of the church today, specifically in Western culture, there is a growing complacency around organizing people to build holistic community for the common good. This complacency is rooted in many different realities including:

Chapter 2

1. **An enslavement to the status quo.** Our own fear of change and aversion to risk immobilize us. Our instinctive response is, "We've always done it this way before," or "This is the way we do things here." We either wilfully ignore the fact that Jesus is doing a new thing or struggle in the fog of our inertia to even see it. When a congregation becomes comfortable with its own status-quo mentality, doors to Jesus's new thing begin to shut. When we give in to inertia and immobilization, to our natural fear of change and risk, we have no energy to be creative, innovative, or intentional about organizing people.

2. **A consumption with busyness and activity.** Activity without a purpose or busyness without clarity around the impact we are seeking to make leads congregations to focus on programs, buildings, and budgets only, rather than investing the time necessary to focus on mission. A church focused on its purpose is constantly examining why they are here, who they need to reach for Christ, how they are going to reach them, and how they will know they are making a transformational difference. Every activity, every program, and every effort is linked to the church's purpose and mission. Churches who find themselves consumed with purposeless busyness and activity either are too exhausted or don't have the bandwidth necessary to plot a strategy for connecting people for a change.

3. **A lack of identity.** Complacency in congregations can also set in because we forget who we are and whose we are. In our Methodist tradition, identity is wrapped up in a Wesleyan theology of grace. This theology, or study of God, presupposes that we love one another unconditionally because God loves us unconditionally. However, our denomination finds itself engaged in an internal fight over who is loved and who is not, which unfortunately crosses lines of race, ethnicity, class, age, gender, and sexual ori-

entation. When we Christians lose our identity, we forget that it is God's church and God's mission that we are to be a part of and that we are to pursue this mission together—as the body of Christ in the world. We give Jesus a bad name in front of people who are searching for good news and meaning in life. When we don't know who we are or when we lose focus of who we are as the church, it is easy to become complacent.

4. **A lack of understanding of how and why Jesus organized people.** Without this understanding, we resort to organizing around cliques, causes, or common interests. While none of these is a bad thing per se, this sort of organizing leads to a country-club mentality, which only increases a group's complacency. Jesus's mission strategy was a risk-taking movement, not a comfortable association with people who could meet the same standards of acceptance. His is a life-changing journey that involves innovative, mission-focused organizing—connecting people for true change in our communities.

Truth be told, it is easy to become complacent. We get stuck in our ways, comfortable with our preferences, resistant to new ideas or fresh approaches. We almost become resentful of growth.

One of the congregations in our district found itself so stuck in the status quo that even when the associate pastor managed to galvanize a group of youth around soccer, the church didn't know what to do with them or the families who came as a result. While a group of youth may sound like a great opportunity and blessing, it only becomes that if enough of the existing church can pray for the new ministry and pay for it, without having to control it. In this congregation, the pastors spent a lot of time trying to educate the long-standing leaders to understand why it was part of their identity as Christians to love their neighbors—especially if they didn't think, talk, dress, or act like them. They preached about love almost every Sunday. They modeled new ways of being in ministry through soccer camps and bringing youth to some district-wide youth gatherings, but still the congregation tried to get the new families to fit into the way the church "does things"—that is, the status quo.

At one point in this congregation's journey, it had more new people in the new worship services than it had in the one service comprised of long-standing members. These new people were from the community in which the church resided and were a different race and ethnicity than the existing members. Over time, the leaders who allowed their identity in Christ to be bigger than their comfort zone were transformed. They were able to fully embrace the new life the church was living into. They are now on the verge of flipping the script on the power structure of the church, giving God's church to the people God has been sending.

Richard Rohr, in one of his popular devotions, said that sin happens when people refuse to grow. That is the danger of complacency.

It is also why throughout Jesus's ministry, we see him shaking people and institutions from complacency around organizing people. He tells the people to "allow the children to come to me.... Don't forbid them, because the kingdom of heaven belongs to people like these children" (Matt 19:14), and turns over tables in the temple, angry that God's house had become a house of trade and not a house of prayer. In these instances and others, we see Jesus passionately persistent in shaking people to the core to stay true to who we are as children of God. Jesus shook people by exposing assumptions, mind-sets, and attitudes around organizing people. In Luke 5, Jesus exposed Peter's spirit of quitting. Jesus takes our failure and tells us to try again. In feeding the five thousand, Jesus refused to accept the disciples not wanting to take responsibility for feeding people. In shaking up complacency, Jesus taught that you must embrace the truth—the uncomfortable truth—even when you might lose people. After he fed the five thousand and walked on water, he sought to shift his followers from being satisfied, eating miraculous bread and fish, toward being organized around Jesus's identity as the Bread of Life. Likewise, we must challenge and expose assumptions, mind-sets, and attitudes that create complacency around organizing people.

Organize People

Jesus taught that you must embrace the truth—the uncomfortable truth—even when you might lose people.

As we cast God's vision on the district, which included the mandate to "claim zip codes for Jesus Christ," shaking off complacency was required. The establishment of connecting elders, the creation of an intentional strategy for charge conferences, and a commitment to equipping and developing leaders in a variety of ways became the strategies we used to support people and churches in shaking off complacency so that they might be freed to move toward the vision.

Connecting elders were clergy leaders in the district who we felt showed passion, promise, and purpose around mission strategy work. Their role was to connect church leaders in a cluster to one another, their communities, and the district by:

- Facilitating relationships amongst cluster pastors and their congregations. This could include (but wasn't limited to) (a) monthly clergy times of sharing and prayer; (b) leveraging opportunities for cluster outreach, prayer, projects, study, worship, and youth engagement, which makes a difference for community engagement and discipleship.

- Assisting in the creation and achievement of annual cluster goals.

- Helping churches in the cluster get outside the walls of the church and meaningfully engage the community through gift and asset mapping, led by the Holy Spirit. This could include (but not be limited by): (a) running a relational 1:1 training and campaign for the cluster; (b) conducting house meetings of like-passioned people to gain further clarity, relationship, and commitment; or (c) involving the cluster in district opportunities and vice versa.

We spent time in regular clergy meetings and church conferences teaching out of Joe's book, *Walking with Nehemiah*,[1] and brought in additional resource persons to help inspire and equip clergy for the task at hand. We sought to do the same in our laity development sessions. We asked clusters to identify who their hearts broke for and to walk their communities to learn more together. These two activities in and of themselves helped shake complacency. In the first year, half the clusters did this while the other half tried to get to know one another.

Another aspect of the district-organizing strategy, which shook people from complacency, involved converting annual charge conferences into church gatherings that focused on two major questions: (1) What are you going to do within your cluster to make more disciples of Jesus Christ this year? (2) What one tangible need in your community or in your zip code are you going to address this year that also helps you build relationships? This strategy moved churches into working on efforts to reach more people with the gospel, grow their ministries, and see what needs they could better meet in their communities—individually and collectively. By any means necessary, shake off complacency!

> What is your complacency rooted in?
> What do you need to do to shake off complacency?

Deepen Commitment

We cannot organize people without commitment. Leaders must have a commitment to organize; others must have a commitment to follow. The word *commitment*, however, in many churches today is a curse word. People don't want to hear it, are afraid to say it, and have conniptions when it is uttered. In many situations, we've almost abandoned commitment. Don't believe us? Ask your congregants to reread the membership vows they took and watch the squirming begin! Churches that are growing and thriving discover that people are looking for a community of faith that walks the walk and talks the talk, which requires commitment! Churches that are struggling and fighting death have often neglected to work with their people to bring them to a deeper level of commitment.

Part of Jesus's skill as an organizer was his focus on deepening commitment. He put energy into connecting people and pulling individuals together for the common good. He did so persistently, intently, sometimes effortlessly even when he was in the presence of those he didn't know very well or who didn't like him very much. Jesus organized people so simply and succinctly around five basic practices to deepen commitment.

Churches that are growing and thriving discover that people are looking for a community of faith that walks the walk and talks the talk, which requires commitment!

First, **Jesus spoke to people's hearts**. He did so by observing people and listening to people so intimately that it did not take long for him to discern what really mattered to someone. From discerning Simon Peter's deep frustration from the empty nets of a failed night's fishing expedition to a foreign woman's embarrassment and shame at a well because she somehow couldn't shake the problems or pain of her past, Jesus could connect with the heart of anyone and then heal that heart with a simple word or command.

We must rekindle this gift in the church today, for connecting with people's hearts is critical to organizing people. Regardless of our partisan persuasions, the Rev. William Barber was right in his speech given at the 2016 Democratic National Convention in Philadelphia, Pennsylvania: "America has a heart problem." Not until we reach people's hearts, can we connect for a change. Jesus shows us that when we get to know someone's heart, we can invite that person to organize around great purposes.

Second, **Jesus called and equipped people, then modeled for them** what he wanted to see in the world. Once he spoke to their hearts, he often called them to something profound. The fishermen at the Sea of Galilee discovered this one day. After a miraculous catch on the lake following an unproductive fishing expedition, Jesus called them to a greater vision, that is, to catch people with the message that broken lives can become whole again. Then he spent three years in an intimate relationship with them, encouraging them to follow him everywhere he went and modeling for them how to heal people, cure people, save people, lead people, and connect people for a change. (He even modeled the importance of spiritual disciplines as a critical part of organizing.)

The church needs to get back to the basics of calling, equipping, and modeling. The kids from Marjorie Stoneman Douglas High School in Parkland, Florida, did that for the nation when gun violence tragically struck their school. They immediately called and equipped people and are still modeling for the world what justice should look like, even against forces that would seek to quiet them.

Third, **Jesus organized people through caring for people's individual needs.** A tax collector named Zaccheus, small in stature and shamed because of his career, found Jesus removing his shame, liberating his home, and compelling his heart to go out into the community and restore fortunes to people he'd previously taken advantage of. A demoniac with mental and emotional issues found himself clothed and in his right mind because of an encounter with the Master. Soon thereafter, Jesus told him not to travel with him but to stay in his community to organize the people around the good news, the message of healing and wholeness.

We saw two athletes—J. J. Watt and Tim Duncan—recently do that in their cities and countries of origin after devastating hurricanes ravaged Houston, Texas, and the Bahamas, respectively. The NFL star and the NBA legend both stayed in their communities and led massive fundraising and food and product distribution networks to ensure that storm-impacted residents were able to acquire the basic needs they had for survival. By focusing their attention on caring for people's individual needs, they were able to mobilize and connect hundreds of people for change.

Fourth, **Jesus communicated to people something greater than themselves**. Sometimes he did that one-on-one, and sometimes in crowds, like the Sermon on the Mount. He started with laying out a way of living that leads to a blessed life. Then he exhorted the crowd to understand their divine role in the world—why we are here. Then he talked about why he was there and centered the crowd in the foundation of the good news: love that finds us in our brokenness and leads us to wholeness. After soaking them in this rich communication, he began teaching how wholeness can play out in our everyday lives, helping us with real-life scenarios around character building, forgiveness, adultery, divorce, and loving enemies—everyday life experiences that people face. And he then organized people by communicating a better way, a greater way of life than what might be our everyday assumptions about what we can and cannot accomplish. Eugene Peterson's translation is direct: "In a word, what I'm saying is, *grow up*. You're kingdom subjects. Now live like it. Live out your God-created identity. Live generously and graciously toward others, the way God lives toward you" (Matt 5:48, MSG).

Tarana Burke, the founder of the Me Too movement, took this characteristic of Jesus personally. She simply made a declaration to herself and others that she and other women no longer needed to be trapped in the silence of sexual abuse. By letting another woman know that she was not the only one, that Tarana herself had also been through it—"me too"—she pointed women toward the possibilities that life could bring by stating the abuse, releasing it from having control over them, and then pursuing the possibilities that relinquishing such guilt could bring. She communicated to people something greater than themselves and then pointed women to it. She has raised countless women up.

And fifth, **Jesus coordinated systems to have their full organizing impact**. One of the best examples of this is found in Luke 10 as he organized the seventy-two:

> [He] sent them on ahead in pairs to every city and place he was about to go. He said to them, "The harvest is bigger than you can

imagine, but there are few workers. Therefore, plead with the Lord of the harvest to send out workers for his harvest. Go! Be warned, though, that I'm sending you out as lambs among wolves. Carry no wallet, no bag, and no sandals. Don't even greet anyone along the way." (Luke 10:1-4)

He then went on to lay out a specific strategy for what they were going to do and how they were to behave in ways that allowed them to discover that they, too, had the power to heal, the power to cast out demons, and the ability to withstand all types of trial. For those with low self-esteem, he transformed them into experiencing divine confidence and positioned them to evangelize cities with the gospel and to expose neighborhoods to his good news through some of the most unlikely vessels.

While these five practices to deepen commitment are laid out one at a time, often we see multiple practices play out simultaneously. For example, Jesus's feeding of the five thousand is an expression of implementing systems that met people's needs, even in the most impossible of situations. He took the complacency of the disciples ("This is an isolated place and it's getting late. Send the crowds away so they can go into the villages and buy food for themselves" [Matt 14:15]) and moved it to commitment ("You give them something to eat" [Matt 14:16b]), which then inspired courage to take what they had and what they could find and organize people for the common good. So good was Jesus at this type of organizing, that in the story of the feeding of the five thousand, people even had leftovers!

The church today can learn a great deal from Jesus about deepening commitment to organize people for the holistic common good. When we commit to speaking to people's hearts, calling and equipping them to model the holistic life that the world yearns for, caring for people's needs, communicating to people something greater than themselves, within systems that can transform, the church will truly be the catalyst that makes disciples of Jesus Christ for the transformation of the world. Our church leaders, congregations, and judicatories must commit to Jesus's organizing principles if mission strategy is to take root.

When we commit to speaking to people's hearts, calling and equipping them to model the holistic life that the world yearns for, caring for people's needs, communicating to people something greater than themselves... the church will truly be the catalyst that makes disciples of Jesus Christ for the transformation of the world.

One of the churches in our district was a cooperative parish with two properties and two separate but intermingled congregations. The leadership had done a wonderful job speaking to the hearts of those in the congregation and community, calling and equipping people to serve in leadership and organizing them around feeding people and becoming a reconciling congregation. When we came on board, they were trying to figure out what their next faithful step was. They had been approached by a developer to sell the property with awkward parking in the middle of one of the busiest intersections in its county in exchange for cash and fixing up the larger (building and congregation) church on a major road on the edge of a residential community.

Instead of taking the money and giving up the only United Methodist presence in that zip code, they worked with us to facilitate a vital merger process that included articulating a vision greater than themselves and a plan for being better together. The vision was: *A movement of Christ's love, feeding all of God's people—body, mind, and spirit—so no one goes hungry.*

With this congregation organizing itself and its community solidly around a common vision for feeding people in every place of hunger so that people would hunger no more, it became the responsibility of the district superintendent's office and our judicatory to invest everything we could to help this vision expand. The goal was to make one campus the worship and education hub and the other a site where mission efforts could be maximized throughout the community, whether they were the initiatives of the congregation or not. Already it was a site that incubated faith communities from various denominations and ethnicities and housed a kitchen. With the crystalized vision in hand, it went further.

What recently emerged was a community kitchen; the collective organizing of the congregation and community partners produced a feeding site where families in need from all around could acquire fresh food to meet their nutritional and financial needs. This is what happens when we shake off complacency and deepen commitment.

> *Where are the places your commitment needs to be deepened? How is your faith community gaining deeper commitment of its participants?*

Be Courageous

Maya Angelou said, "Courage is the most important of all the virtues because without courage you can't practice any other virtue consistently."[2] Many would argue that we live in times in which courageous leadership is needed more than ever, particularly as it pertains to organizing people for the greater good. We are a divided nation, and we are not practicing the virtuous values upon which this country was established. Global relations are on edge because of the shifting cultures experienced in many countries across the world.

Fear is out here. It's ugly. Many people are afraid to organize because of the price that might be paid for organizing. If there was ever a time when a courageous decision to build bridges of common unity and understanding across lines of difference was needed—even when we differ on the particulars—now is that time.

When Jesus sent people out, he knew they would need to be courageous to put what they had experienced into action for themselves. Perhaps that is why he commissioned and sent them out in pairs. He did not send people out by themselves because perhaps he knew that if one person fell, that person had no one around to help her or him. Instead, he sent them with the biblical organizing principle that two are always better than one and that where two or more people come together on anything, then anything in the name of Jesus is possible.

When mission strategizers come together with this mind-set, truly anything is possible. But it requires courage. It takes faith to see what is possible and courage to risk chasing after it. Martin Luther King Jr. is famous for saying, "If a man [or woman] has not discovered something he [or she] will die for, he [or she] isn't fit to live."[3]

Karl Barth, the famous theologian, was noted for saying, "Courage is fear that has said its prayers."[4] Courage isn't just about taking the first bold step, but about continuing to take bold, uncomfortable steps toward God's prefered future. Congregations build a culture of courage by intentionally deepening commitment, celebrating learning and progress along the way, and consistently focusing on their mission. A meaningful, shared focus on the mission field is essential. This focus needs to be understood both poetically and practically. It should be both inspirational and measurable in real time. In the church, often we have an inspirational "goal" (e.g., love God and neighbors) without an accompanying shared understanding of what that looks like. Collective courage is easier to muster and maintain if a group of people agrees and believes in why and how it needs to take bold action and what that action should look like. A shared sense of purpose, a shared understanding of how we will be moving toward that purpose, and a shared sense of progress toward that purpose support courageous leadership only if progress includes learning from "failure" or pivoting (scrapping an initial plan for a better plan). Too often the very systems we create for healthy accountability and shared understanding become straightjackets or fear factories that shut down innovation and courageous action.

A group of courageous young adult leaders came together in Washington, DC, to organize people to be innovative. Through our research, we discovered that 35 percent of the residents in the District of Columbia—which has rapidly become one of the top five most expensive cities in the country—were young adults, with an average age of twenty-six. Yet, most of our congregations were not reaching this expanding young adult population, nor did they have a strategy for doing so.

> **Too often the very systems we create for healthy accountability and shared understanding become straightjackets or fear factories that shut down innovation and courageous action.**

So, we organized a group of people who we thought might have a shared passion for reaching this mission field, with support from Path 1, our denomination's agency focusing on new church starts. We designed a "young adult planting zone." We wanted to support and strengthen congregations reaching young adults, but we also wanted to be courageous and strategic in creating ministry possibilities across the city that would engage young adults whom the church was not reaching.

This meant we had to take risks. We had to spend time in unfamiliar neighborhoods. We had to create opportunities to meet new people across racial, ethnic, and sexual-orientation lines. We had to form new relationships with young adults who were college grads and those who hadn't finished high school, those who were upwardly mobile and those who had a criminal record. And we had to bring these emerging leaders together with leaders in the church who had a common mind to see what might be possible if we dared to connect for a change.

The first phases brought excitement and resistance. Many pastors of established churches balked behind the scenes and out loud at this new initiative that just might affect their ministries. But what also emerged was a set of young leaders, many of whom were active in church, who saw that young adults could be engaged strategically if we looked at the various entry points where young adults might get connected to a faith community. This set of leaders began to focus on organizing small groups with an eye toward building worshipping communities and service opportunities—feeding people, tutoring kids, providing affordable housing for those who are homeless or working poor, and developing a training ground for young emerging leaders. These leaders gave their initiative a name: InspireDC.

Our first steps sprung up quickly, although we faced challenges and even lost a few leaders to illness and relocation. We connected people across the area who were all trying to do the same thing in different spaces, that is, to maximize resources, to share ideas, and to provide encouragement. InspireDC grew to become a network of people organizing around the same purpose: reaching, growing, and multiplying young adult disciples through service and justice.

And through this organized effort acting courageously, the following happened:

- We worked with a church to establish a third worship service to reach a younger population from a different racial background.

- We renovated a part of a formerly closed church building and used it as a base for feeding people and as a site to partner with a fledgling new church start from a Wesleyan tradition to reach people in a neighborhood that was the youngest in the city.

- We established a ministry called FEEDS that partnered with DC Campus Kitchen to provide hot meals to people all across the city. We saw food deserts gain some abundance.

- We started building a coalition around affordable housing.

Not all of these elements are still in existence, but the spirit of them are. Organized people who are courageous can connect for a change, bringing hope to otherwise hopeless situations. But the efforts must be ongoing and sustained. Generating revenue is critical, as is the painstaking, regular process of building relationships and organizing people. In order for courageous leadership to continue, leaders must be patient, prayerful, and persistent.

Chapter 2

At first glance, courage and patience don't seem likely to coexist, but any situation that requires courage requires patience because failure will happen. Roadblocks will appear. And there will be many times when determined, courageous leaders will want to give up. Risk-taking can exhaust us, and sometimes we won't see the fruit from our labor. Risk-taking can demoralize us, when people or circumstances beyond our control destroy ministry that required so much to build. This is where spiritual maturity and a deep foundation of prayer are needed.

Jesus set a great example of this for the church and the community. As the Son of God, Jesus often found himself in the midst of massive crowds with massive needs to be met. Each challenge required courage and required him to be at his best. He mastered these challenges because he never forgot the importance of getting alone with God, praying, and receiving strength to face the next challenge. This was a consistent pattern for Jesus that is easy to see in Matthew 14: challenge, retreat to a deserted place; challenge, dismiss the disciples on a boat and climb a mountain to pray; challenge, get alone with God; challenge, rise up in the wisdom and strength that only solitude with God can provide. This is how patience and persistence in the face of seemingly insurmountable challenges is possible.

It can be done in the most impossible of places. The Washington, DC, metropolitan area, where we serve, is one known for its deeply rooted and sometimes above-ground racial divisions. These divisions were systemically created, have deep history, and cross so many lines of survival and abundant living across the city. They are educational and financial in nature. They have involved laws and policies in housing, education, and financial institutions that have kept people of color "down," while creating broad opportunity for the dominant culture. And with massive gentrification now being the visible reality across the area, the racial divisions are being greatly played out with regards to average median income, renting versus buying property, public versus charter versus private education, neighborhoods of preference, and so on.

As the church, we can be complacent around this issue, too. One side can say, "We have ours. We don't need to be bothered with 'them.'" The other side can complain about real injustices, but never move to do anything about it. And those in the middle can be paralyzed from moving in any direction because the issue feels too big and complicated. One side can keep injustices going simply by the policies we create and enforce; and the other side can be the victim of these injustices, often having to work so hard to survive that fighting back is not an option because of lack of time and energy.

But we initiated, encouraged, and witnessed people organizing around racial justice and reconciliation in our district. When Michael Brown was assassinated in cold blood on the streets of Ferguson, Missouri, the call went out to leaders in congregations to have a conversation about what was happening in our country. Close to two hundred people assembled on a cold, rainy weeknight two weeks before Christmas to begin creating winnable movements that could build bridges across the racial divide. From this, groups in the city and the surrounding regions began organizing to inspire changes in local governments, school systems, and churches. Even congregations of different racial backgrounds and checkered racial histories started coming together to heal the wounds of the past so that a bright movement forward could be created. When organized people are courageous, impossible things can happen.

Where are you being called into risk-taking mission?

Chapter 3
Utilize Assets

Ministry without utilizing assets is like a sports car without a country road. Like a lamp without anything to illuminate. Like a human without purpose. When we don't utilize our assets, we miss the greater possibilities for ministry, and we are usually consumed by scarcity thinking. Too often our people, churches, and judicatories complain about what they don't have instead of discovering, celebrating, and using what they do have. Too often our people, churches, and judicatories forget the assets in our communities and our congregations. Even if you are building relationships and organizing people, you can't do mission strategy well without a clear sense of the assets within and outside of the church. Where assets are unknown, God calls us to discover them. Where assets are unappreciated, God invites us to take a kingdom view. Where assets are utilized for the common good, God's economy is revealed.

Uncover the Unknown

Sometimes an asset is unknown because we do not know what an asset is. An asset is someone or something that can be positioned by God to bring blessing to an individual or group of people, or to a situation, or circumstance. *Mission Possible: Design Thinking for Social Change*, developed by Matroyshka Haus (an organization of faith-based missional entrepreneurs) provides a fun and instructive way of discovering the role assets play. Each team is given three random assets from three out of four categories (because we are rarely given everything we think we need). The simple asset categories are human capital (skills/time/numbers), facilities (buildings and spaces), money, and equipment. These asset cards contain such things as one hundred mason jars, three antique bikes, a football field for a day, two hours of graphic design, pro bono legal work for twenty hours, and the like. It is amazing to watch teams figure out how to use these simple assets to address a part of a real-world problem (e.g., poverty, alcohol abuse, hunger). They leave the game surprised and energized by the amount and variety of assets around them.

Sometimes we literally find ourselves sitting on our assets! When I (Joe) was sent to pastor Emory United Methodist Church in Washington, DC, I found myself leading a congregation with very few financial resources: a very old, declining building and property infiltrated with multiple signs of marginalization and broken lives. People used to tease us, calling our building and our congregation "the mausoleum on the hill." Little did they know, and little did we know, that we had assets! We had a faithful few (people) who wanted to see their congregation and community revived. We had land—valuable Washington, DC, square footage. Those assets have enabled a vital congregation to emerge. The "mausoleum" has become a beacon of mission-focused change.

For years, Emory had searched for ways to address Washington, DC's number one problem: the lack of affordable housing. This problem is the result of gentrification, rising property values and a skyrocketing cost of living. We saw the problem close-up in the people who were sleeping on our church steps each night. We discovered that because of air rights, we could use our asset of land to provide a solution. Lo and behold, we were sitting on the asset that was most needed! The people of Emory and community partners developed a $56 million housing project on the land surrounding our church. Now nearly three hundred people have an affordable place to live. Stop sitting on your assets!

Interestingly, an asset doesn't always take on missional meaning until the part of the problem you are seeking to solve is clarified. One of the best examples of this is found in Jesus, who in the midst of teaching experienced the problem of more than five thousand very hungry people. And so, to emphasize the missional meaning of what he was teaching, Jesus asked his twelve disciples to address the problem before them. The people were hungry and needed to be fed. He instructed the disciples to deal with the problem head-on instead of running from it. He asked them the question, "What do you have?" forcing them to look for assets around them. He believed and knew that the disciples possessed some asset that could help resolve the problem.

Stop sitting on your assets!

Jesus taught his disciples—and teaches us—to assume that there's always a fish sandwich in the crowd. There's always an unknown asset that can meet someone's need and resolve someone else's problem, that can connect people for a change and bring hope to people's despair.

Leaders of mission strategy *must* have a loaves-and-fishes mentality. From 2007 to 2008, I (Christie) was the project manager for the Romans 12 project.[1] The study was initiated by the General Board of Discipleship of The United Methodist Church in order to discover what differentiated a church that thrived in its holistic witness from one that did not. Various contexts (such as size, setting, race/ethnicity, socioeconomic area, location within the United States) were explored to come to the necessary conclusions. A part of the study included an intensive weekend visit to learn what we could from these thriving congregations. In each visit, interviewers found a loaves-and-fishes mindset woven through the DNA of the congregation. Lay and clergy leaders consistently described how they identified needs and how God provided for those needs.

Chapter 3

Leaders of mission strategy *must* have a loaves-and-fishes mindset.

As we were comparing notes, we observed that there was a strong expectation that God would meet needs after diligent prayer and work. We came to understand that leaders in prayer, who replaced their scarcity mentality with an abundance mentality, were able to share stories of God at work again and again.

Getting rid of a scarcity mentality can be a challenge for many. This type of mentality consistently focuses on what we don't have (versus what we do have) and makes it very difficult to see things and people as assets. This "lens of scarcity" colors everything and can lead to hopelessness, fear, defeat, desperation, and depression. Furthermore, a scarcity mentality pours cold water on divine vision and deflates transformational hopes and dreams. Scarcity mentality also prevents holy collaboration as it drives people to compete as if there is only a little piece of the pie available to us. Yes, resources can be limited in many situations, but what defeats us more than anything is having a mindset that is limited—a mentality that does not see that little can become much when we put it in the Master's hands.

When we begin working with leaders on mission strategy in their context, it is normal for them to talk about what isn't working as they lay out the problem they are seeking to solve. If they have a scarcity mindset, several things happen at the same time. First, the conversation centers on examining the problem rather than searching for a solution. Second, people can't see a way out of the problem. Third, they think they don't have or can't get what they need to resolve the problem. And fourth, they spend an inordinate amount of time talking about "why we can't" instead of "this is how we can." So, statements such as "because we don't have ____, we can't thrive" become prevalent. If you are tempted to fill in the blank for your context (*We don't have enough money. We don't have a young enough pastor. We don't have any young members.*), you might be suffering from a scarcity mentality!

An abundance mentality, however, sees that all things are possible with God. This mentality recites over and over again that eyes have not seen, ears have not heard and neither has it entered into the hearts of men and women the great things God will do for those who love God. This mentality is in the hearts of people who dream big dreams and see massive visions, and are not afraid to chase after them regardless of the many costs that are involved.

While an abundance mentality comes naturally for some, for others, it can be learned. None of us has to walk around stuck in a scarcity mindset. Mike was a lay leader at one of the churches we worked with who naturally operated with a scarcity mentality. When we first interviewed him, he even said as much: "I'm the curmudgeon in the crowd who doesn't see the silver lining because I'm worried about the clouds." Even though he affirmed the leadership the new pastor had brought and the fact that more people were attending worship than had in the last ten years, he was filled with reasons why the church wouldn't be able to take the steps necessary to thrive. If we were talking about strategies to improve financial strength, he would counter by saying, "We have been spending our savings for years and—even though our new pastor is bringing in new people—we still have a deficit." If we were strategizing about what to do with the parcel of land the church owned, he would interrupt the process of exploring ideas to state: "We've had many different architectural plans on the shelf for years. We simply don't have the will—or ability to raise money—for building out."

In preparation for a discernment retreat, leaders were asked to use a process called SOAP. SOAP is an approach and acronym taken from Wayne Cordeiro in *The Divine Mentor: Growing Your Faith as You Sit at the Feet of the Savior*.[2] Leaders were asked to read a chapter from the book of Acts a day and then reflect/write on four aspects:

S—Scripture   Write one verse that stood out to you.

O—Observation   Write what you see in the verse and surrounding section.

A—Application   Write how you sense God wants you to apply this verse to your life.

P—Prayer   Write a short prayer of response, asking God to help you do what God just showed you.

Mike was the loudest complainer about this being given as an assignment prior to the retreat. We asked him to trust the process and told him that those who actually did the assignment would be much better positioned to participate. At the retreat, Mike showed up with an entirely different demeanor. Through the SOAP exercise, he glimpsed an abundance mentality, perhaps for the very first time. He shared just how life changing that had been. He had experienced God speaking through the living word and prayers being answered. This allowed him to open himself up to possibilities in ways he hadn't been able to the previous sixty-four years of his life. Because of his shifted mindset, he was better able to collaborate with others even as he continued to provide his gift of grounding us in the current facts.

Living with an abundance mindset says there's enough out here for everybody, and if we do it God's way, there's more than enough for everybody.

It's important to say here that abundance thinking is different from a prosperity gospel. Abundance thinking actually helps put prosperity in its proper perspective. *Prosperity* means to "help another along the way." When we help others along the way, we aren't just helping others; we're living into our shared divine purpose. Like the good Samaritan, we demonstrate loving our neighbors in concrete ways and, in doing so, experience a form of worship. Living with an abundance mindset says there's enough out here for everybody, and if we do it God's way, there's more than enough for everybody.

When leaders live with an abundance mindset, their congregations are better at recognizing and utilizing their assets. We worked with an African American congregation that found itself surrounded by a wealthy, white community. The community didn't used to be that way. There was a day when the neighborhood was entirely African American. But as happens in many cities, the last thing to change in many neighborhoods is the church. And this church found itself as no exception.

While other African American congregations in the neighborhood left and became strong, or stayed and died, this congregation stayed and sought to remain vital to the neighborhood. To survive and thrive however, the people in the congregation had to decide what sort of attitude to adopt, now that their neighbors didn't look like them and their parking spaces had disappeared. Would they mope and complain? Or would they examine their assets and do something with them?

They decided to do the latter. First, they discovered that one of their hidden assets in the neighborhood was the people on the street who were homeless. In an attempt to help this population, the church raised money to renovate its kitchen and to turn the fellowship hall into a place where those who are homeless are fed on a regular basis. Second, in spite of a painful racial past in the neighborhood, the church decided to reach out to people in the community who didn't look like them to ask them to join the church in serving. Third, the church began to partner with other churches in their community to share in this ministry of feeding the homeless. One of those partners was another United Methodist church in the neighborhood. These two churches had a divisive history; the black church members separated from the white church members because of racial discrimination. Through partnering to meet a common need in the community, the two churches began reconciling old wounds, repenting from past actions and behaviors,

Chapter 3

and moving forward on one accord. Through each of these actions, what appeared to be a hopeless situation for a declining congregation became a ray of hope and holy imagination for what God can do and what can be when we uncover the unknown.

What scripture builds your abundance mindset?

Value the Underappreciated

Oftentimes all the assets we need are right under our noses, but we fail to appreciate their fragrance. We can be looking at these assets for years and never see their true value. An asset becomes an asset when we view it as such and when we allow it to be all that it can be. What if God already gave us everything we needed to achieve God's dream through us? Perhaps you are wondering why God isn't answering your prayers when there's a great possibility that God has answered them already. Don't underappreciate your assets; value them!

The prodigal son in the New Testament unfortunately had to learn this lesson the hard way. When we meet him, it appears that he had everything he needed to live a full life. He had his father who provided everything he needed, he had his family for support, and he had an inheritance at his disposal. He lacked for nothing. But he underappreciated what he had and ended up squandering it because he did not value it. His heart was not in tune with God, the plan God had for him, and the assets that God placed before him to make it happen. When our hearts are not in sync with a kingdom-building mindset, it is very easy to be blind to, or to underappreciate, all that God has already placed around us.

Many years ago, my (Joe's) mom told me her version of "Acres of Diamonds." A man, discontented with where he lived, spent years trying to move to a more desirable neighborhood. After what felt like an eternity, he finally convinced an unsuspecting family to buy his house. The man leaped for joy, for he was finally leaving the hellhole he thought he was in.

Weeks later, he got an unexpected call from the family. They excitedly told him about what happened when they went to plant a garden in the backyard. As they tilled the soil, they stumbled across a glittering object. They kept tilling, and more glittering objects began to emerge. They stooped down to see what these objects were, only to discover that they were diamonds! And as they kept digging, they discovered that their entire property was filled with diamonds. They were literally living on acres of diamonds!

When the previous owner heard this, he wept. For he realized that he never bothered to uncover his assets and fully appreciate what he had and work with what he had. He was too busy looking at something else rather than looking at what God had already blessed him with.

Both the man who sold his "acres of diamonds" and the prodigal son were looking for something other than what they had. This belief that "the grass is always greener on the other side" causes us to underappreciate and miss out on assets in our midst. Unlike the man who sold his property, the prodigal son received a second chance. He "came to himself," the story goes, and returned home as humble as he knew how, to tell his father how much he valued him. The father restored him and even gave thanks for the asset he had in the son who had squandered so much in riotous living.

When we pause to value the underappreciated assets around us, great things can come to pass.

Sometimes underappreciation happens because we are over-appreciating something else. Leaders can get stuck in the rut of over-appreciating their own ability to make ministry happen. This over-appreciation can result in feeling overwhelmed, feelings of inadequacy, loneliness, and arrogance. I (Christie) was working with a leader of a church that had grown under her leadership, but had reached a stagnation point. In preparation for an upcoming retreat for church leaders, I asked her questions to try and get a sense about what might be valuable for us to focus on. When I asked what the most pressing issues were, she said—with exhaustion in her voice—"What isn't pressing? We have recently rolled out our new vision and strategic areas of focus. Each area is in need of new leadership because I can't do it all. For example, we reorganized our Sunday school and I'm not sure the director has fully bought into it; and she is struggling to find teachers who will live into our new vision. I have sat down with each leader and explained the vision and plan, but I honestly don't think we have the right leaders in place to make this happen." When I asked her to describe a leader who she felt was doing a good job, she thought for a minute or two and said, "Honestly, I just don't think I can keep this up. I know that people are trying to help, but it feels like it is all up to me to make this work." She was an extremely gifted leader with God-sized vision who experienced "success" as a turnaround pastor (someone who takes a dying congregation and revitalizes it). This was her second turnaround assignment and she was feeling the pressure.

We made the decision to put the leadership retreat on hold, and the pastor executed a three-fold assignment:

1. Identify the few things that she had to do.

2. Answer the question: if the congregation and its community could talk what would it say that it needs?

3. Inventory who might have the giftedness, passion, and spiritual maturity to help meet the congregation's and community's needs—inside and outside of the church.

Once she identified the team—and acknowledged that she really couldn't do it alone—she was able to take a deep breath and regroup. She "came to herself." And then she was able to value the assets God had put in her midst and was able to allow the team to help create the plan for deepening vitality. Through assessing the gifts and passions around her, she was able to refocus and rebuild momentum that has led to some significant ministry growth.

Utilize Assets

We encourage leaders to inventory all of their assets including potential partnerships. Sometimes in order to do that, leaders must stop over-appreciating themselves and actively seek to discover the priceless nature of relationships, networks, and social capital. For example, InspireDC, mentioned earlier, discovered the power of networking in the food-recovery world. Because they built a real relationship with their local food bank, the food bank introduced them to a network of various companies that were seeking to donate food and individuals and organizations who were trying to identify outlets for the excess food they discovered. This valuing of our partnership led to feeding twice as many people with a reduction in food expense.

Leaders must stop over-appreciating themselves and actively seek to discover the priceless nature of relationships, networks, and social capital.

Sometimes congregations don't view something as an asset until we get clear enough about what part of a problem we are seeking to solve or what opportunity we are being called to seize. Several of our district churches are members of a fifty-strong church, synagogue, mosque, and labor union organization in Washington, DC, called the Washington Interfaith Network (WIN). This group adheres to the Industrial Areas Foundation model of community organizing but also follows other asset-based mapping strategies to maximize the opportunities around us.

One of the great accomplishments of WIN over the twenty-three years of its existence has been mobilizing congregations to create more than 480 affordable places to live, with more than 700 in the pipeline. Perhaps even more important than the construction of these homes were two major things: (1) identifying affordable housing as a great need for so many in the District of Columbia through one-on-one relationship building, and (2) organizing people who many in the city underappreciated because of their race and economic and education levels. These individuals, once they were "valued," became the driving force and the organized voice to bring about change.

Some of the affordable housing units constructed were townhomes targeted to lower-income residents in the city who were threatened with displacement because of constantly rising property values. When masses of people from all walks of life and from private and government sectors of the city joined their cause, suddenly an impossible dream of owning an affordable home became a reality for many. And interestingly enough, when the housing market crashed in 2008, no more than two of the 150 families in these homes had to foreclose on their property. Value the underappreciated asset!

Valuing the underappreciated asset means that we have to take a fresh look at where we are with many of our congregations and communities and really do some serious praying, fasting, and relationship building in community to see what God may be saying anew and how God might be calling us to this new, kingdom-building opportunity. If we take the risk with God, great things can happen!

What would change about your ministry if you believed you already had everything you needed to pursue God's preferred future?

Maximize Utilization

Only when assets are truly appreciated will we be able to steward them well. And when assets are stewarded well, the common good is expanded and even multiplied.

Jesus demonstrated this vividly and powerfully in the parable of the talents, one of the most popular parables in the Bible. A man was getting ready to go on a journey, and before leaving, he summoned three of his servants. One servant received five talents—a talent being a significant measurement of money—another two talents, and the last servant one talent. Each of them received talents according to their ability to do something with them.

Utilize Assets

While the man was away, the servant who received the five talents immediately went to work with his five and produced five more talents. The servant with the two talents did the same and produced two more talents. But the servant who received one talent didn't put it to work, but instead dug a hole and buried the talent in the ground.

Eventually the man came back to settle accounts with his servants. The man saw what the servants with the five and two talents did and was so happy about it, he gave them many more responsibilities relative to the extra talents they had generated. However, the servant who buried his talent endured the man's wrath because of his disobedience. And what the servant had was taken from him, because at the very least, he could have put it in the bank to make interest.

Jesus made it clear that the more assets we steward well, the more responsibility we are given to steward. While the talents in the parable are financial assets, they are representative of any asset the Lord provides. Leaders have to be able to see the possibilities with what they've been given and then get to work for the Lord.

I (Joe) don't know if I've ever been to a place where assets were maximized in more profound ways than in the churches and communities in the country of Zimbabwe. Once the "breadbasket of Africa," Zimbabwe has struggled mightily in the last twenty-five years because of the AIDS epidemic, droughts, political strife, and an economic downturn. However, even with very little financial resource, their maximization of human assets is amazing.

Churches were planted in communities with a just a handful of laypersons who had a vision for spreading the gospel of Jesus Christ in the neighborhoods where they resided. A congregation would typically start in someone's home through what longtime Methodists used to call a "class meeting." The class meetings would grow, and then leaders from the meetings would construct a map of the community, identifying the families who lived in each house. Then a plan was made to visit every house, every family, with the intent of building a relationship, offering people Jesus Christ, and inviting them to become a part of their faith community.

Chapter 3

On the map, leaders identified which families had said yes to Jesus and yes to joining the fellowship, which families offered themselves as assets to reach other families, which families said no and didn't need to be approached for a while, and the like. While they didn't have the assets of slick and massive marketing campaigns to reach folk for Christ, they did have the assets of their legs and feet to walk door to door, their hearts and voices to declare their personal testimony of the goodness of the Lord, and their tremendous spirit of hospitality to invite people to the opportunity of a better life in Jesus.

Time and again the use of human assets in this strategy led to more class meetings in people's homes, and then, when a critical mass was built, corporate worship was organized in the community. Sometimes the Sunday gatherings were under trees, with people walking to worship in spite of the elements. Sometimes the gatherings were on the loading docks of a local industry in town. Sometimes the gatherings were on a corner lot, donated by someone in the newly formed fellowship or acquired by a church, where "lean-tos"—a structure of boards, sticks, branches, and an aluminum roof, over and around a dirt floor and benches—served as the initial church building.

As these persons stewarded the little bit they had, God kept giving them more assets to bring about the common good, more human, physical, financial, and other assets. Soon, lean-tos gave way to brick structures—structures that were built not by contractors per se, but with the hands of people in the community forming an assembly line and passing down one brick at a time. Sometimes the brick structure would sit roof-less for a while because the roof was the most expensive part of the building. But before too long, the buildings would be complete because the people saw and internalized what Jesus has taught us, that the more assets we steward well, the more opportunities are presented. Not only were these assets used to build congregations, but also they were used to feed people and to educate children who could not afford school fees.

Reverend Tim Warner, a pastor in my conference, and I went to Zimbabwe for a mission trip. We were doing follow-up on church projects that we'd partnered on with the Zimbabwe United Methodist churches. We paused on one day of our trip to visit a school that our bishop at that time, Felton May, had helped to fund. The school was named Ishe Anesu, meaning "God is with us" in Zimbabwean Shona language, and its goal was to educate as many kids as possible in a community called Sakubva, which was one of the poorest communities in the country. These kids could not afford school fees, and because kids going to school in Zimbabwe required uniforms, you knew the kids who were poor.

Tim and I went to visit the school to see how things were progressing. On this one occasion, the director of the school said they were coming along, but needed a kitchen. So many of the kids came to the school, she said, not having had anything to eat. Tim and I asked how much was needed for a kitchen. We were told anything we could give. We had a total of seventy-five US dollars in our pockets at the time and gave the director that amount. That was in the morning. When we came back that evening, the kitchen and an outdoor structure with appropriate covering had been built, and biscuits were being cooked by the mothers in the community for the children, to our amazement. Along with the school children, we sat down and ate the first fresh biscuits from the kitchen. That was more than fifteen years ago. To this day, the outdoor wooden structure still stands, but it stands next to a fully furnished brick structure and kitchen that can feed many more students. And the graduates of the school, who go off to higher endeavors, come back to teach those whose shoes they once filled. The more assets we steward well, the more opportunities are provided.

In the United States, most pastoral leaders coming out of seminary will be sent to a congregation that either requires a turnaround or needs to be revitalized. These congregations are like "talents." They will have assets, but they may not be assets in the best of shape. There will be people who have endured struggles and buildings that are in significant disrepair. But they will be assets just the same. The question becomes, *What will these pastors and lay leaders and congregations do with what they have?* Will they get to work and make the most of it? Or will they bury it in the ground?

Chapter 3

Congregations need to focus on maximizing the asset of leadership—the most important asset to develop.

Congregations need to focus on maximizing the asset of leadership—the most important asset to develop. There is a faith community in Tampa called Underground Network started by InterVarsity leaders who got tired of watching their on-fire graduates being asked to sit in pews and tithe, instead of continuing to grow as church leaders. The driving force of Underground Network is simple: to get people to recognize God's voice and to understand what God is calling them to do. They have launched more than two hundred micro-churches (small missional communities) and several networks since their inception in 2008. They are maximizing the asset of leadership and constantly calling people to leadership and fully embodied ministry. They are focused on creating "a missional ecosystem designed to support and serve missionaries to plant microchurches.... For the past decade, Underground Network in Tampa has equipped leaders for God's mission, served the poor, and reached the unreachable. Everything we do is aimed to unlock the church's potential to create an empowering missional culture to send and serve lay-missionaries."[3]

This is one of the best examples I (Christie) know of maximizing the asset of leadership. Underground Network sees everyone as a potential leader and has a holistic understanding of discipleship. I went to its annual conference one January and experienced how its Sunday morning experience was different from what we traditionally call worship. Network members call it the Crucible and view it as weekly conferences to equip micro-community leaders and members to take the next faithful step. While subtle, the shift is life changing. In our denomination, we tend to set measures around the percentage of worshippers who are in a small group (which may or may not include a component of service/mission/social impact). Underground Network is all about the missional community and providing resources for those missional communities to grow (deepening in discipleship and launching new leaders).

In more traditional contexts, this maximizing of leadership also needs to start with the notion that everyone is a potential leader—a missionary in the non-colonialist sense of the word—and include clear leadership pathways and processes so that we are developing disciples who lead others, lead leaders, and eventually lead movements, if that is where God is calling. This type of leadership development resembles some of the dynamics inherent in the parable of the talents.

1. Support people in discovering their God-given gifts (talents) and help them explore where to invest them. This can be done in a myriad of ways from regular classes to new-member classes to coaching to discernment processes. Just be sure that you provide ample support for people to explore using their gifts right away. Knowledge is necessary, but not sufficient for transformation.

2. Give assignments based on spiritual maturity, risk-taking, and fruit rather than time spent on the pew or as a member. Too often, when we think about who might be a good leader, we think about the same people over and over again, or we think about people who have been with us for a while. There is nothing wrong with that, except you could be valuing longevity more than calling or demonstrated potential, and miss your blessing.

3. Create the expectation of discipling and apprenticing relationships—that is, discipling at least one person and being discipled by at least one person.

4. Recognize leadership isn't just about the people who "run" the church (buildings, finances, logistics, and personnel) but about the people who "are" the church. One of the most common practices in healthy churches is to celebrate and elevate small-group leaders. Why? They want more of them. Most small groups are designed for accountability, encouragement, learning, and application. In the case of Underground Network, small groups also involve compassion and justice as well.

5. Don't stop developing people. When I (Christie) first heard the parable of the talents as a child, I wrote in a subtext: that the two-talent person was given five talents the next time and the five-talent person was given ten talents the next time. Later in adulthood, I thought that perhaps we each have a God-given capacity and that we are to risk 100 percent of that capacity for the common good. At this point, I can testify to the fact that people rarely know their worth and as soon as one stops growing, one starts dying. Let's be on the expectant side of vitality. Let us be blown away by the amazing things God does in and through imperfect people. Let's encourage people in our midst to give it all for God.

Which of the five levers above do you need to focus on next to maximize your leadership assets?

Maximize the utilization of assets!

Chapter 4
Liberate Congregations

Ministry without liberation is like a car that thinks it's a bicycle. Like a lamp that only turns on when it knows the person who is turning it on. Like a human that isn't aware that he or she was made in the image of God. Without liberation, our congregations struggle to know who they are and whose they are—and struggle with thinking beyond themselves and fulfilling their role. We can build relationships with wonderful people, organize people in meeting tangible needs, and use the very best of our assets for the common good. However, if we forget that our main purpose is discipleship that liberates people so that they have life and have it to the full, we miss the mark. We cannot do mission strategy effectively, for there is no mission without this type of discipleship. This type of discipleship must be actively lived out in our congregations, or we will continue to be viewed by the world as irrelevant. The fact is, congregations must be freed from the trappings of doing church so that they can be the church in a world in need of God's grace. Where congregations are locked up, God calls them to a different reality. Where they are loosed, God positions them for a greater witness in new ways. Where they are launched into new possibilities, they are able to free others from oppression.

Chapter 4

Without liberation, our congregations struggle to know who they are and whose they are—and struggle with thinking beyond themselves and fulfilling their role.

Illuminate the Lockup

Liberation is only possible when a congregation can admit to its own bondage. This can be a very difficult process. Some churches have been locked up for so long, they don't even know they are bound, like an elephant that gets used to being chained to a stake in the ground and still walks in the same circle even when the chain is gone. From churches that are scrambling to fill slots in leadership, to those who are arguing about what music should be played in worship, to those that are fighting about the same things and people that they've been battling over for years, the "lockup" can be intense. Even churches that aren't struggling can find themselves just going through the motions, which is a different form of being locked up. The way out is to first acknowledge this situation.

Many churches today are operating out of a membership and building mind-set instead of a discipleship mind-set. Decisions and conversations tend to be focused on maintaining the operations, programs, and budget of a church and keeping its members satisfied, rather than on intentional ministry to transform lives for the good. The building, budget, and programs should all be in service to the mission, purpose, and people who God is calling us to bless.

When we work with churches, one of the first questions we ask leaders is where they think they are on a version of George Bullard's life cycle of a church as simplified by a colleague of ours, Andy Lunt.[1]

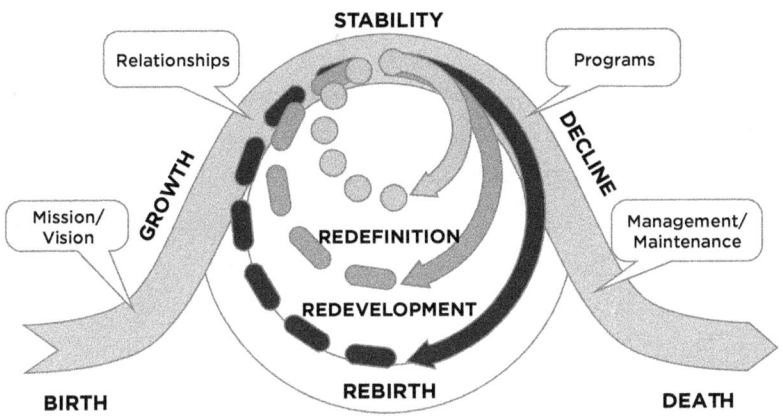

We talk about how, like a human, a church is born and—if it survives—grows rapidly until adulthood. Then it plateaus for a while until it ages and starts a rapid or gradual decline. Unlike a human, a church can decide to be reborn. Depending upon when the church realizes it is in decline, this represents more or less work. For example, if a congregation finds itself spending the majority of its time and energy on programs, it needs to ensure that programming is intentionally advancing the mission of liberating souls and building relationships with new people. In this way, the church can continually reevaluate and redefine its ministry to keep it fresh and relevant. If a church is further down the decline side of the curve, it must engage in ministry redevelopment. Redevelopment includes mission strategy work—such as building new relationships, learning what the community is crying out for, and discerning how God wants to use the congregation. If a congregation has been in decline for many years, the rebirth cycle is required. This is very difficult work. It means, in effect, becoming a new church, one that is vigilant about its God-given mission and purpose of liberation.

This exercise forces congregations to identify the nature of the lock up and then to wrestle with how to get back to the main thing. In the midst of

Chapter 4

those conversations, inevitably one or more leaders will say something like: *The reality is that there's just so much energy to go around. By the time we attend all the meetings, plan all the programs, troubleshoot the building issues, encourage stewardship, deal with issues and drama that come up, there's no time left to think about new people or our mission.* If you resonate with this sentiment or feel like you are going through the motions or caught in the whirlwind of ministry, you are locked up.

Liberation can come when you take a step back from the whirlwind of ministry and figure out what to focus on so that new and more spiritually mature learners and followers of Jesus emerge. In The United Methodist Church, the mission is to make disciples of Jesus Christ for the transformation of the world. Faith communities need to define and unpack this in their context. John Wesley had some pretty clear ideas about the holistic practices—individually and communally—that form disciples who love God with all their hearts (soul justice) and love as Jesus loves (social justice). Wesley's Rule of Discipleship reflects the nature of this: "To witness to Jesus

Christ in the world and to follow His teachings through acts of compassion, justice, worship, and devotion under the guidance of the Holy Spirit." This results in a rhythm of holistic discipleship that forms and defines individuals and faith communities.

Additionally, conversations around the life cycle tend to illuminate more misunderstandings of what the church is and isn't. In every church, there are some people who have always had their primary focus on the building (what goes where, who does what, and so on) and don't see how that could lead to decline. For them, the church building is the main thing. The building needs to be understood as an asset for liberation, not an object to be worshipped. The building's purpose is to be used in fruitful ways even if it's not the existing congregation who is using it. We must always remember that the church is the people, not the building!

The building needs to be understood as an asset for liberation, not an object to be worshipped.

Jesus taught the disciples (his congregation) that we must always keep our focus on the main thing. Congregations (people) often lose sight of the main thing: liberating souls and society from bondage so that people can live life and live it to the full. Instead of focusing on the main thing, we can get caught up taking sides or getting lost in theological debates. But when we focus on the main thing, we can accomplish our mission: healing and hope, liberation and life for people in our community.

Jesus best illustrates this in the story of the man born blind in the ninth chapter of the Gospel of John. The story opens with Jesus seeing a man who has been blind since birth. Jesus is with his disciples (the congregation) who see the man as well, and his disciples immediately get into a theological discussion. They want to know who sinned, the man or his parents. Jesus immediately lets them know that the main thing is not the sin or who to blame for it. The reason for the man's condition is to be able to see the works of God in and through him.

In other words, the man is in his present test so that one day he might be a testimony to the world that Jesus is able to liberate anybody from anything. We church people tend to focus on discussions that ultimately mean nothing to the liberation of a soul or society. We need instead to focus on the possibilities all around us for living life and living it to the full.

Where do you or your congregation feel locked up?

Our denomination has been divided for years because we've been "locked up." We cannot even find ourselves on one accord around who Jesus is, what Jesus is about, how Jesus is contextualized in our present-day culture, and what Jesus can mean for us individually and collectively. We struggle with what it means for Jesus to be "Savior and Lord" for us. We are alright with Jesus in our church buildings, but we are confused about what it means to live with him and follow him in our everyday lives.

Some of us have the understanding and embrace a "Hollywood Jesus"—a white, wavy-haired Jesus who is gentle and kind and has violins playing behind him in a safe and secure environment. Or we think of Jesus as the image that Warner Sallman painted that was so prevalent in many of our parents' and grandparents' and great-grandparents' homes—the image of Jesus as soft, smooth, and very European. We will add scenes of his crucifixion to make him look tougher and even portray him theatrically in plays like *Godspell*, but we wrestle with applying the biblical Jesus to our everyday lives—in the classroom, in the corporate boardroom, in community, and in the confines of our own homes.

Others of us study scripture and discover that Jesus was not white but a person of color. Bronze, if not flat out black. His hair was woolly, and his back was constantly against the wall, and the only way out, as the renowned theologian Howard Thurman puts it in his book, *Jesus and The Disinherited*, was to live like "the Kingdom of God is within us."[2] We understand that

Jesus's mission was to give sight to the blind, proclaim good news to the poor, and set the captive free. But because we struggle to have a common understanding of who Jesus is *now*, and what Jesus is about in our context, we take sides in theological discussions based on our own perspectives; we dig in and double down, energetically defending our positions. We lose sight of the main thing, which is our mission to continue Jesus's mission. This behavior runs deep and is at the root of our "lockup."

Is your or your congregation's understanding of Jesus at the root of your lockup?

It's wreaking havoc in the church and world today. Racism is real, and it divides us. So much so that we don't want to discuss it or deal with it. We instinctively look the other way, even as unarmed, young black males continue to be gunned down in the streets by rogue police officers; as Latino children are locked in cages, separated from their parents who came legally seeking asylum; as the Black Lives Matter movement and its work for justice is attacked unjustly; and as politicians legislate division between races and ethnicities.

Jesus is trying to tell the church that theological differences and discussions and side-taking are going to be there; they are not going anywhere.

United Methodists are so divided over sexual identity that in 2019, we convened a special session of our global church meeting to discuss and decide our future as a denomination. The meeting was in St. Louis, Missouri, a city known for its racial tension, which borders the town (Ferguson) where the shooting of Michael Brown took place, in a state that is on the top-ten list of the most dangerous places to travel for people of color. We met as a denomination, not to take action to heal the racial divide, but to hash out a decision over who is sleeping with whom and what role certain people should have in the church, when all of this stuff and so much more is already happening in the church. We are locked up.

Jesus is trying to tell the church that theological differences and discussions and side-taking are going to be there; they are not going anywhere. But the main thing is how can we eliminate the oppression that people are experiencing, how can we liberate oppressed people from bondage, how can we liberate the oppressor from oppressing, how can we live in truth so that the truth can set us free. How can the test that we're in, like that of the blind man, become a testimony? What if, instead of digging in, doubling down, taking sides, and guarding our positions, we focused on Jesus's main thing? What if we worked single-mindedly to end oppression and to bring peace to people's lives?

The nature of the institutional church, including congregations, is not even to see the blind man. Our nature is to walk past people in these predicaments because we either don't have time or think their condition is their problem, so they should deal with it, not us. Jesus illuminates our "lock-up" by seeing the man and then stopping to figure out how to liberate him. And he models for the church what it is he wants to see. If we are going to be like Jesus, we, too, need to model what Jesus wants to see as confirmed by his word, and as church leaders we must position other leaders, congregations, and communities to experience and offer liberation like this.

And, as we see in the text, it doesn't require an outlay of cash, nor does it require a massive social service agency. While both of these assets are sorely needed to meet the significant needs that emerge from poverty and disenfranchisement around the world, Jesus shows us that in many situations, these assets can be conserved and used more wisely. While we are writing a check to deal with an issue, how are we also reaching out in the discipline of love, in practical, person-to-person ways? Illuminate the "lockup!"

What bondage is your faith community in?
What do you need to illuminate so the lockup is clear?

Let It Loose

Oftentimes God has made it clear that what used to work doesn't work anymore and if we keep trying to make it work, we will stay locked up. The old adage still rings true: insanity is when we do the same things we've always done and expect different results. At some point we have to shift. If you aren't getting the results or having the impact God wants you to have, you need to release what no longer works; let it loose and let it go.

Jesus sought to get his disciples and those around them (his congregation) to shift in John 11. In the chapter, he offers us another model for how people and congregations can experience liberation by releasing what no longer works. As the story unfolds, his dear friend and brother Lazarus becomes sick in his hometown of Bethany. Mary and Martha, Lazarus's sisters, send word for Jesus to come and heal him, but Jesus delays his arrival to show his "congregation" how God "lets loose" or liberates in order to set people free.

Lazarus dies, and Jesus arrives after the three-day period in which "tradition" believed resurrection could happen. Jesus is greeted with the mourning of Lazarus's sisters and their disappointment that he came late to the scene. Both sisters tell him that if he had come earlier, their brother would not have died. But Jesus, filled with faith and not fear, informs them that their brother will rise again.

A significant part of loosening congregations from a "lockup" condition is encouraging congregants to believe that release is possible. If there is a culture of doubt and disbelief, release will be very difficult to experience. But when there is a movement emerging that says in word and deed that release is possible, new things become possible.

And most of the time, it takes just a remnant of enthusiastic leaders in a congregation, lay and clergy, who believe that liberation is possible, for it to happen, leaders who believe that Jesus is "the resurrection and the life." We have experienced this in numerous churches in our district, sparked by laity who "got it" and the appointment of clergy who believed against all odds that when Jesus is present, great things can happen.

Another significant aspect of releasing what no longer works is confronting the major issue causing bondage. In Jesus's and his congregation's case, it was confronting the central matter that was keeping them from liberation—believing that Lazarus' death was the end of the story. In the early church, Paul specialized in helping congregations confront their central issue that was causing them to be locked up. For example, Paul confronts the church in Corinth about its divisiveness particularly over the issue of spiritual gifts.

It is one thing to illuminate that which keeps a congregation locked up in bondage. It's another thing to confront the bondage in such a way where release from its control can take place.

Congregations must ask and answer honestly and transparently, "What is keeping us mourning and lingering in this dead situation?" When the situation is illuminated, we must have the courage to confront it without fear and then address it with faith and courage. To let it loose, congregations must understand that fear must be released. So often, we do not tackle our "lockup" because of fear. But as the apostle told Timothy, God did not give us a spirit of fear, but a spirit of power and love and a sound mind.

We simply have to release what no longer works to be able to discover what can work!

In one of the churches in our district, the pastor and the congregation were being locked up by the control of one family. The family controlled the decisions on big issues including property use and on other moves regarding money. What they said was how things went. What they did was how things rolled. The control this family wielded over this congregation was remarkable and had gone on for years, with those who chose to stay in the congregation subjecting themselves to this bondage.

Liberate Congregations

Over the years, this congregation dwindled significantly. But after a new pastoral appointment and a series of internal leadership shifts, change began to happen. The pastor and a handful of members recognized the situation surrounding the family and, through prayer and discernment, confronted it by faith and with courage. A team of three wrote a new financial policy and the church council approved it over the loud protests and threats by the family, who realized this would erode their control. There were friends of the family who understood the dynamics of the situation and who sought to provide emotional support for them for the transition. God began moving the dead situation out of the way. And, now the congregation is moving forward in profound ways—ways in which it hadn't moved in decades before. Sometimes God is simply waiting for one or two or three people to show some courage, confront the dead situation, and believe that, in the name of Jesus, tombstones can be taken away and the possibility for life can emerge again. Once we show the courage, God takes control. We simply have to release what no longer works to be able to discover what can work!

Another significant aspect of letting it loose is a congregation calling back to life that which appeared to be dead. We were once called in to work with a congregation in serious chaos and conflict. The church had turned on its pastor, who was struggling with being ineffective, and members of the congregation had begun to turn on each other. There was no effective discipleship strategy for the congregation, and many people had left or were contemplating leaving. The pastor lost trust in the congregation, and the congregation had lost trust in the pastor. We intervened to address the problem through an intensive assessment process that illuminated death and life in the congregation, while the pastor's supervisor addressed the appointment issue that was critical to the life of the congregation. The strategist worked with a team to call the congregation out of its death spiral, to let it loose from the bondage of unresolved conflict, mission drift, and wrong priorities. We offered a few next steps and decision points, and we coached the leaders and congregation to let go of the negative behaviors and practices that bound them, so that they could experience the vitality and joy in ministry once again. This is the very pattern of Jesus's encounter with Lazarus.

It may appear to be contradictory advice, but in order to release what no longer works, leaders must focus on the possibilities and not the problems. If you let it, ministry can become an endless stream of problem solving. Ministry leaders face many problems: too few reliable volunteers, diminishing worship attendance, interpersonal conflict, building issues, and on and on. Leaders who see everything as a problem to be solved or a situation that needs to be fixed not only experience more stress and less joy in ministry, but also can get trapped in the it-is-up-to-me-to-fix-it box. This box simultaneously is draining, can get in the way of helping others to develop and grow, and sometimes shuts God out. We were working with a very capable lay leader who had been active in leadership for thirty years in her local congregation. She had served in every single seat of leadership and was a trusted confidant of each pastor who had served that church. She was relentless about "cleaning up" each area that she led, and with each new assignment, it seemed that people were more and more happy to watch her work. Thirty years later, she was describing for a team all the various things she had tried to do to get more people involved in ministry and to grow the commitment and skills of those who are already serving.

One of the newer leaders on the team provided gentle feedback that moved the conversation away from a focus on the problem to the opportunity that loosed idea sharing and increased energy. He shared his surprise that she had been seeking to solve the problem when he thought all the "join us" messages were just an invitation and not a need. It seemed that from where he sat that the ministries were running just fine. Perhaps, he continued, they actually had an opportunity to help people find their place of serving that helped them deepen their discipleship and grow in their call. This simple shift created a huge difference in how the team began to think and work with one another to improve their collective ministry. What might you need to frame as a possibility and not a problem?

Gary Keller and Jay Papasan offer a key question that creates focus and shifts people from serial problem solving to possibility thinking. In order to get results they ask: *What's the ONE thing you can do such that by doing it, everything else will be easier or unnecessary?*[3] This one question helps individuals identify their strategic sweet spot. Change the *you* to *we* in this question, and it becomes a helpful clarifier for a congregation—as long as it is linked to the congregation's mission: *What is one thing WE can do such that by doing it, everything else will be unnecessary in making world-changing disciples?*

In this era of constant demand for our time and attention, there has never been a greater need to let loose the history of programs, meetings, and "must-haves." Congregations need to do less for more impact. Even though it is a simple statement, there are actually two parts to it that need to be understood: *less* and *impact*. Too often we have a negative reaction when we hear the word *less*. In the Western world, we have a bias toward *more*. And in our work in local churches, it seems obvious to us that churches are seeking to do more with less. Congregations with less than twenty active people are trying to keep up the programming they had when the membership could afford a full-time pastor (and they often want their part-time pastors to work/behave as their favorite full-time pastor worked/behaved). Churches with two hundred to four hundred active participants behave as if they are churches with thousands of active participants. Less for more impact is very different than less for diminished impact. This leads us to explore the other word in the "do less for more impact" mantra: impact.

Impact is about what good looks like in your context. Impact is about how we define and describe the transformation we are seeking to make within ourselves, our churches, and our neighborhoods. As we have talked with leaders from across the church, we have come to understand that churches don't have a clear handle on what impact looks like, let alone how to measure it so that the things that they are tracking help them learn and make better decisions. Impact is not synonymous with activity. Yet too often activity is what people and faith communities name when we ask about impact. Until we identify the impact we are seeking to make clearly and in real time, it is very difficult to stop the hampster wheel of activity.

What are the activities or programs you are seeking to hold onto? A particular ministry? A particular altar style? A certain way of doing communion? A newsletter? An outreach effort? A building?

Release what no longer works. Release those things that aren't creating the impact that you are seeking to make. Release is liberation.

What is ONE simple thing your faith community can do such that by doing it everything else will be easier or unnecessary?
What does your faith community need to release?

Launched to Love

Even when a church or group of leaders have encountered Jesus and done the hard work of getting free from what shackles them, they may not know the next steps to accomplishing the mission of our Lord Jesus Christ. They may be confused about what this new life looks like, struggle with what their current and future realities should be, or even find themselves trying to copy what they think a liberated church looks like.

Simply put, a liberated church is a liberating church that is constantly creating an atmosphere within itself and with its community where new expressions of life-changing encounters with Jesus Christ take place. It looks like one that is launched into everything that the church is really supposed to be about: to love and be loved as Jesus loves, to remove oppression and usher in peace, and to help people become whole—physically, mentally, emotionally, spiritually, relationally, financially. It looks like a ministry committed to discipleship that liberates souls and society so that life can be lived and lived to the full. It looks like a congregation grounded in prayerful expectancy that God is going to do a new thing, in new places, with people from all walks of life, wherever we may be. It looks like people surrendered to the movement of the Holy Spirit, prepared to go wherever the Holy Spirit leads and do whatever the "ruach" leads us to do to be the visible example of love in people's lives and communities. But there's some work that people and congregations need to do constantly and consistently in order to look like this.

Jesus discovered his own loosed congregation needed to do this work. And he revealed to them that when they were willing to be repositioned by the Christ, and then reconnected and recommitted to the Christ who's about to do a new thing, they would be launched to love people in ways they and others had never imagined. Dionne Warwick was famous for singing, "What the world needs now is love, sweet love. It's the only thing that there's just too little of."

John 21 gives us a picture of Jesus's disciples (the congregation) having been liberated from sin and disconnection from God by the crucifixion and resurrection of Jesus Christ, but not fully aware of what that meant. Jesus has even shown himself risen to the disciples on three occasions. Yet still, the disciples, in fear, uncertainty, and confusion, aren't quite sure what all this means or what's next.

Peter suggests that the congregation go fishing, that it return to what it used to do and how it used to be. That is the trap that even liberated congregations must be careful of—doing things like we used to do them. But Jesus reveals to the disciples rather quickly in the text that once we've been liberated, we cannot go back to how things used to be. If we do so, we will come up empty in all of our efforts.

Instead, we must reposition ourselves for a new thing. Because in the new thing, the possibilities of our reaching people with the good news of Jesus Christ and by the power of the Holy Spirit, leading them to a liberated life, are endless. Following Jesus's command, Peter repositioned himself and his disciples on that lake. And the catch of fish was so overwhelming that, again, like in Luke 5, he needed help to haul in the catch.

Chapter 4

Unless we remember that we've been blessed to be a blessing, we will miss the mark.

But the work does not end with repositioning. Repositioning can find us basking in our own blessings, but not positioned to fulfill the mission of loving people unconditionally. That's what liberates souls and societies. So often, congregations bask in our own blessings. But unless we remember that we've been blessed to be a blessing, we will miss the mark.

So Jesus calls us, like he called Peter, to a time of reconnecting and recommitting. Reconnecting and recommitting with Jesus enables us to be fully surrendered to what must and what will be, even if it means doing ministry in places where we do not wish to go. What must be is that Peter and others in the congregation understand unconditional love. That's why in the reconnection and recommitment, Jesus asks Peter, "Do you love me?" three times. He wants Peter and his congregation to know that the love that Jesus is launching them out to display to the world, is a love that loves in spite of every barrier, every division, every challenge. And that when people see this kind of love demonstrated to them in the most difficult of times, then they will come to experience the liberation that only Jesus provides all by themselves. That's what Jesus teaches Peter and his church as John 21 comes to a close and the book of Acts is introduced. Jesus reconnects with Peter to let him know how deep unconditional love is and must be and leads him into recommitment because he and the others are about to be launched into a mission of loving—unconditionally.

Our churches need to reconnect and recommit to Jesus like this. For we live in painful and hurtful times of division, dissension, hate, evil, and malice. Times in which the gospel needs to seep into places where and people to whom we do not wish to go; unconditional love needs to be the rule of the day.

This is the work of the liberated church: asking "What's next?" and allowing the Holy Spirit to answer. To liberate congregations of liberators requires us to be empowered by the Holy Spirit because unconditional love in its fullest effect cannot happen without souls who have been captured by the Holy Spirit. This encounter with the Holy Spirit requires us to develop the discipline of waiting on God, working to be in the same place, at the same time, with the same frame of mind with people who seek a healthy, holistic life for themselves and all people.

When the Holy Spirit blows through a congregation, a liberated church that is a liberating church begins to speak a common language in church and community. Not a language of division, but a language of unity. Not a language of separatism, but a language of welcome. Where we can speak a language that does not cause or create social chaos, but one that honors diversity and directs people to living a whole life. There is true koinonia, oneness, and an authentic picture of people loving unconditionally, being engaged in bringing about the salvation of souls and the common good.

We were recently at a Fresh Expressions US conference and heard one pastor describe the struggle his church was having around trusting people to try new forms and methods of disciple making. He described how much some influential church leaders were struggling with the notion that one of their members created a "ministry" with a group of people who didn't go to their church. This group was meeting in a home of someone who was not a church member, and it was growing in size and ministry, but none of these new people were "joining" the church. The spiritual leader of this group was a lay member of the church and was feeling pressure from the organization to "bring those people" to church. These well-meaning church members didn't understand that the church had left the building and had taken up residence with people who otherwise would not be in contact with the Living Word. They didn't understand how much they should be celebrating the fact that one of their members had deepened her discipleship and was creating a pathway to discipleship for others who wouldn't ever (or weren't yet ready to) set foot in a building that looked like a church.

Chapter 4

The pastor went on to explain that much of the conversation ended up revolving around clarifying for the church which ministries they "own" and which ministries they "bless." This, in a nutshell, describes the line that must be crossed when moving toward true liberation. Until leaders and congregations really accept the fact that the church belongs to—is owned by—God and not the leadership team or administrative council or the people who are paying the most amount of money to keep the church doors open, there will always be artificial understandings and barriers that limits what the church can and cannot do.

It reminded me (Christie) of something that had happened at a recent event designed to give participants a taste of missional innovation at the intersection of church and social enterprise. At the end, one gentleman stood up and said: "This has been a great day! I have received confirmation about what God is calling me to do, but my church won't let me do it." After all the other speakers had given him great advice on how to pitch his idea, I encouraged him not to let gatekeepers define his reality. I advised him to find two or three people who saw the vision and would work with him to make that vision come to life.

We can testify that if a spiritually mature leader is following the leading of the Holy Spirit and it is confirmed by others—whether or not those others are also in the church—great things will happen.

So, leaders, who or what do you need to bless?

In the stage of launching congregations, we have to stay connected to timeless traditions even as we are transcending the forms we may have grown up with. This is helped by maintaining deep connection to the mission of the church, stewardship, spiritual maturity, and how the Holy Spirit functions. Without these things, a congregation will not truly be free.

1. **Mission**

    Hopefully by this point, the reader understands that the mission of the church is not to get new members. The mission of the church is to co-create and develop disciples who love as Jesus loves. The church is Christ's bride. The mission of the church is to join with Jesus in fulfilling his mission: "The Spirit of the Lord is upon me, because the Lord has anointed me. He has sent me to preach good news to the poor, to proclaim release to the prisoners and recovery of sight to the blind, to liberate the oppressed" (Luke 4:18 and referencing Isa 61:1).

2. **Stewardship**

   We do not own the church; God "owns" the church. Read that again and reflect on how often battles are fueled by our misunderstanding of ownership. Church leaders are stewards of time, talent, and treasure, which means—once we have illuminated our places of bondage and death and released what we need to release—we must make good decisions about how to invest the resources under our care. This requires clarifying what we are actively managing and what/who we are releasing and blessing with no strings attached. This may mean making difficult decisions like not spending down the endowment but handing it over to the next generation to lead.

3. **Spiritual Maturity**

   Age or time spent in the church doesn't correlate to spiritual maturity. We have met church members who have attended Bible study for decades who show no fruit of the spirit. Eugene Peterson describes this fruit in his translation of Galatians:

   > But what happens when we live God's way? He brings gifts into our lives, much the same way that fruit appears in an orchard—things like affection for others, exuberance about life, serenity. We develop a willingness to stick with things, a sense of compassion in the heart, and a conviction that a basic holiness permeates things and

people. We find ourselves involved in loyal commitments, not needing to force our way in life, able to marshal and direct our energies wisely. (Gal 5:23-23 MSG)

Spiritual maturity is developed through a series of practices and decisions that result in us being permeated in oneness. Spiritually mature leaders are essential for full liberation because of the difficult discussions that are required and because they can discern what is the wind of the Holy Spirit and what is hot air.

4. **Holy Spirit**

   The Holy Spirit isn't theoretical, but practical: it resides in us and is our source of power. Charles Stanley's eleven attributes of the Holy Spirit demonstrate the nature of this power as explained in scripture: it convicts us of sin (John 16:8); permanently indwells us (John 14:16-17); seals us (Eph 1:13); teaches us (John 14:26); guides us into all truth (John 16:13); reminds us (John 14:26); bears fruit through us (Gal 5:22-23); comforts us (John 16:7); equips us with spiritual gifts (1 Cor 12:4-7); fills us (Eph 5:18); and empowers us (Acts 1:8). Liberation is not possible without this power being acknowledged, leaned on, and trusted.[4]

What ministries are your faith community called to manage, and what ministries are you being called to bless with no strings attached?

Chapter 5
Inspire Hope

Over the course of this book, we've been looking at four basic multipliers for how faith communities can engage people, churches, and partners to inspire hope in their neighborhoods and communities, connecting for a change to bring about the common good. We are living witnesses in our work as mission strategists that when we build relationships, organize people, utilize assets, and liberate congregations, powerful and profound things can happen, and people can live life and live it to the full.

We have shared our living testimonies to this work and explored lessons from the life of Jesus and others. As we seek to wrap it all up, we turn to the book of Exodus, which provides undergirding for mission strategy and the four multipliers. Specifically, in Exodus 18, Moses is seeking to bring holistic change in the lives of people literally walking through the wildernesses, the valleys, the deserts—in other words, the challenges of life. The people Moses was interacting with were in that place of being liberated, having been set free from Egyptian bondage, but not knowing what it meant, why they'd been set free, where to go, or what to do next. They knew they were heading toward a land of promise. They knew they were seeking to get to a place and space in their lives where they could live life and live it to the full. But they needed divine guidance and godly direction—hope—that would enable them to live in healthy community and navigate life's challenges. So, they came to the only one they knew who could provide a way through these challenges: Moses, Yahweh God's chosen servant leader.

However, Moses, unbeknownst to him, was burning out. His leadership style in this situation was causing him and those he served growing dissatisfaction. About that time, Moses's father-in-law, Jethro, shows up to reunite Moses with his wife, Zipporah, and their two sons. Jethro is the priest of Midian, a believer in God almighty; and upon reuniting, he and Moses begin sharing all that God has done to deliver the Israelites, God's congregation, from Egyptian bondage and from the hardships the congregation has experienced along the way.

Shortly thereafter, Jethro observes a day in the life of Moses and quickly realizes that the way Moses is leading is not sustainable. He offers Moses a better way, a model for mission strategy so that Moses and the people can be healthy and effective as they journey through the wilderness to the promised land. This way is offered to us as well.

Check Your Leadership Style

At first, Moses seeks to work this mission strategy all by himself. From morning until night, he meets with people trying to resolve their wilderness issues. But the model for mission strategy that Jethro offers does not require that we work ourselves into exhaustion, but that we work wisely with all of the resources we've been given.

Jethro informs Moses in Exodus 18:13-27 that trying to do mission strategy as a lone ranger is not good. A lone-ranger mentality burns out a leader and stifles the giftedness of other people who are available to lead—if only the leader would recognize, invite, and allow them to lead. When we don't build relationships and utilize assets that God has placed in our midst, we wear out ourselves and others around us. In doing so, we can become the causes of decline and death in our congregations and communities.

A lone-ranger mentality burns out a leader and stifles the giftedness of other people who are available to lead.

One person cannot do it all, shouldn't be expected to, and shouldn't be allowed to. Not the pastor and not an individual in lay leadership. Yes, somebody's got to lead it. Joe led it as district superintendent; he was the chief mission strategist for the Greater Washington District, spearheading transformative work in this area of the UMC's Baltimore–Washington Conference. But it could not have been done without Christie, who supported Joe and another DS in serving as regional mission strategist for two districts. And it could not have been done without a faithful, dedicated, hardworking district administrator, Olivia Gross. And it could not have been done without connecting elders and key laypeople who brought their gifts to support the mission.

How many clergy and laity are burning out today? How many churches are facing the threat of closure? How many judicatories are throwing their hands up in the air and resorting to selling church buildings for money? How many communities are suffering because we haven't connected people for a change with a mission strategy that engages people, churches, and partners to inspire hope in our communities?

A leader who does not pray is a leader who cannot lead.

Our advice to you: seek out your Jethro. People inside, but perhaps outside your current social or professional circles, have been blessed with great wisdom, insight, and knowledge. Get to know them. Build relationships with them. Listen to their advice. God speaks to us through community. God often confirms the very things we need through community. Thank God that Moses built a healthy relationship with his father-in-law.

Praise God that the in-law was not an outlaw! Moses listened to Jethro and hope suddenly appeared on the horizon.

Know Your Role and Do Your Job

Moses was to (1) represent God to and for the people, (2) teach people the word of God, (3) model what mission engagement looks like, and (4) identify and position leaders.

(1) *Represent God to and for the people.* Jethro said: "Represent the people before God. You should bring their disputes before God yourself" (Exod 18:19). Moses was to hear causes and then lift them to the Lord in prayer. Our chief leaders in particular need to know how to pray. For many of the matters we face—from racism to discrimination, human trafficking to drug addictions, domestic abuse to family division—will only be reconciled through spiritual breakthroughs that begin in prayer. A leader who does not pray is a leader who cannot lead.

(2) *Teach people the word of God.* In Exodus 18:20, Jethro went on to tell Moses that he was to instruct God's people in how life was to be lived and how life could be lived to the full. The chief mission strategist and the strategists around her or him must be teachers rooted in the word of God. In the vast and numerous obligations that bishops, superintendents, pastors, and lay leaders have, paramount within all of them must be the commitment to teach and to instruct people in the Way.

(3) *Model what mission engagement looks like.* Eugene Peterson's second half of Exodus 18:20 states Jethro's advice as "show them how to live, what to do" (MSG). As their chief leader, Moses was to model the word of God and mission strategy for the people so that they could see the teaching lived out. It is critical that leaders walk the talk. Rev. Jesse Jackson puts it this way: "You can't teach what you don't know, and you can't lead where you won't go." The reality is that people pay far more attention to what you do than what you say. The truth is that authentic discipleship is caught from being discipled more than taught theoretically.

Without a leader modeling, it is very difficult to team well and to raise the next generation of leaders. Modeling mission strategy—building relationships, organizing people, utilizing assets, and liberating congregations—is in the job description of mission strategists at whatever level they serve.

As leaders pray, teach, and model mission strategy, people will learn, more strategists will be raised up, and more people will be blessed.

(4) *Identify and position leaders*. In Exodus 18:21 Jethro tells Moses to look "for capable persons who respect God. They should be trustworthy and not corrupt. Set these persons over the people as officers of groups of thousands, hundreds, fifties, and tens." In order for Moses to follow this wise advice, he would have to use his mission strategy skills—building relationships, organizing people, and utilizing assets—where a leadership structure could be developed that would liberate people from situations and circumstances that sought to keep them in bondage and prevent them from living a whole life.

Moses was not to choose just anybody. He was tasked to recruit. And like a great college recruiter or a professional scout, he was to find the very best leaders he could find and likely asked many people to help him discern who was ready. Those with ability. Those who revered God. Those who were trustworthy. Those who were not greedy or selfish or not in it for themselves. And he was to organize them based upon their ability and the assets they brought to the table. Because some would have responsibility over thousands, others hundreds, others fifties, and still others tens. And then he was to liberate them such to where they felt and knew that they were empowered to carry out the task given to them so that others might be liberated. The challenges we face in the world today—like the challenges Moses faced—are too great for us to handle by ourselves. But when we assemble an effective team, the problems of the soul and society can be dealt with effectively.

Chapter 5

Complex challenges are why we assembled connecting elders in our mission strategy work who were each given clusters of churches to lead and be in ministry with. The clusters were a variety of shapes and sizes based upon geography and other considerations. We couldn't do it all by ourselves! It's also why we took the time to discern in our district who could join us closely in this work, taking the time to build relationships with and utilize the human assets of key people we could trust, who could advance the cause when we were not always around. Without these individuals, congregations could not experience liberation and lives could not be blessed.

Stay in Your Lane and Trust Others to Lead

With the mission strategy coming to life before them, Moses would then hear Jethro clearly define the lanes in Exodus 18:22: "Let them sit as judges for the people at all times. They should bring every major dispute to you, but they should decide all of the minor cases themselves. This will be much easier for you, and they will share your load." After clarifying Moses's role and job, Jethro emphasizes the fact that the real work would be letting them make it easier for him. In order for this to work, he—and we—have to stay in our lane and trust others to lead.

As the superintendent and chief mission strategist, Joe handled the major cases—from appointment issues, to clergy care, to pouring into the district team and connecting elders, to responding as major cases came to light, and so on—and Christie, Olivia, and the connecting elders handled the matters necessary for implementing the strategy across the district and managing the day-to-day. As Jesus demonstrated with his three and twelve and seventy-two, there is wisdom and power when we are attentive and intentional about the leaders we are pouring into or apprenticing. In our case, we did this with three on the district team, twelve connecting elders, and seventy-two faith communities (sixty-six churches, three new faith expressions, and three campus ministries).

As long as those leading with you share a passion for the vision, revere God, are trustworthy, and lead others with integrity and effectiveness, you must trust them to lead in the way God has designed them to lead.

Essential to this is not only having the right people on the bus, but also having clearly defined seats and ever increasing trust and communication so that everyone's contribution is valued and confusion is minimized. When one is in charge—the buck stops with you—it can be difficult to trust people to lead in the area you are ultimately responsible for. Particularly so when other people have leadership styles different from your own. But the question here isn't style; rather it is integrity and effectiveness. As long as those leading with you share a passion for the vision, revere God, are trustworthy, and lead others with integrity and effectiveness, you must trust them to lead in the way God has designed them to lead. This requires honesty and real conversation. Part of the reason Moses and his people wandered in the wilderness for forty years is that the leadership team wasn't together.

Stick to the Plan

Peterson describes the last part of Jethro's advice as follows: "If you handle the work this way, you'll have the strength to carry out whatever God commands you, and the people in their settings will flourish also" (Exod 18:23 MSG). For us, we sought to handle the work the way Jethro laid it out and saw leaders, congregations and communities flourish.

We have been told by conference, jurisdictional, and national leaders that our district was a key model for growth in the last two of our three years of serving—numerically through church attendance increasing, financially through apportionment gifts rising, and enthusiastically through more leaders presenting themselves in their communities to lead. We truly believe that this growth was because of connecting people for a change through mission strategy and grounding people, churches, and partners in the hope that comes through it. This hope resulted in two church plants and growth that, outside of the districts representing the state of West Virginia, was the highest of any district in the Northeast Jurisdiction. We share this information to testify about what can happen for anyone when mission strategy becomes the focus of their work.

Mission strategy is an essential discipline.

In carrying out God's mission, leaders, congregations, and people will experience hardships along the way. We will be liberated from certain situations and feel like we are still in bondage with others. But God is faithful and God will deliver. God always points us back to holy strategy—revealed through God's word—that leads us to live life and live it to the full.

Mission strategy is an essential discipline. And when we dare to connect people for a change—through building relationships, organizing people, utilizing assets, and liberating congregations—our churches will be alive. Our communities will be revived. More and more people will experience liberation in their souls and in society. And the enemies of disconnection, division, distrust, and disbelief will be defeated. Isn't that why Jesus came? Isn't that what grace and love in action produce? Isn't that what we really are to be about?

May it be so.

Appendix

Tips for Judicatory Leaders

Judicatory leaders, those charged with governance, need to work toward becoming proficient in the four multipliers of mission strategy (chapters 1–4) personally, before attempting to use these tips. You can't be at the beginning stages of these multipliers and think that you will be able to do effective strategy in your mission field. This section presumes that a judicatory or denominational leader is at least in the growing stage in most, if not all of the multipliers, and it provides tips, learnings, and ideas that are essential for being successful at mission strategy.

Building External Relationships: Community beyond the Church

When a judicatory leader begins to look at his or her mission field, he or she will naturally see the pastors, congregations, and other judicatory leaders as people and as entities with whom he or she needs to build relationships. These are clearly essential relationships. However, in order to be effective at mission strategy, a judicatory leader must also learn how to build relationships across the three major sectors that make up any community whether it be urban, suburban, rural, or something in between.

These sectors are private, government, and public. Simply put, the private sector brings money into the community and drives the economy of the community. The government sector is responsible for legislating, establishing, and maintaining order within the community. The public sector is made up of everyone else: people and organizations who live, move, and have their being in the community. The effective mission strategist understands that he or she must build relationships, organize people, utilize assets, and work for liberation in each of these sectors while understanding how each sector works and how to position the church so that the church can be the catalyst for community, connection, and change.

Organizing People: Growing Clusters of Churches via Connecting Elders

It is important to identify those congregations who are relevant to their communities and ask those leaders—lay and clergy—to help organize for good. As described previously, we couldn't have been successful in the cluster strategy without the right connecting elders. Even having the right people, we learned that each cluster had its own time line for formation and fruit.

Some of our clusters thrived, and others struggled to find their rhythm. The clusters that thrived had a couple things in common: (1) the pastors valued the idea of being connected and didn't feel in competition with one another; (2) the congregations had shared passions (e.g., youth, Hispanic/Latino ministry, service). Where these two factors were present, cluster charge conferences set the pace for the year ahead and provided a tangible experience of how we are better together as people of faith.

After twenty minutes of worship and thirty minutes of business, the remainder of the time was spent evaluating where the cluster was and goal setting for the next year. They came up with shared goals and worked toward them. Talk about shaking up the status quo! There were some clusters who did only superficial connection, but by the end of the three years, all but two of the clusters were at least providing spaces for clergy to support and encourage one another.

The more deeply rooted congregations were in their identity, the easier it was for fruit to be born out of the cluster. The expectation of cluster growth helped keep before congregations a healthy tension about whose church it was and clarified that the focus was on the mission field. It also revealed which churches were stuck because of busyness and status quo. Many laypeople thanked us for shaking things up and providing room for new expressions of church to happen; these same people had been trying to convince others in their congregations to do things differently for years.

It took much longer for clusters with part-time pastors to form. This was simply a time issue. We noticed that clusters without a full-time pastor in their midst had a very difficult time figuring out when and how to connect between district clergy meetings. In the first year, some of our clusters were too big so we subdivided them to facilitate better relationship building. After the second year, we made some changes so that there was at least one full-time clergy person in each cluster.

In our work in clusters, we found that many different stages of commitment were needed. If left to their own devices, busy congregations will seek to meet a district expectation of mission strategy by simply doing something together, which may or may not be something that the community was longing for. We get it. We really do. We are all seeking to do less for more impact. The commitment to do this beyond a single congregation can be asking a lot.

We have learned the following about the hierarchy of commitment on a district level:

- **First, there must be a commitment to pastors meeting monthly.**
  Without healthy relationships among clergy, the healthy relationships among congregations become much more difficult.

Additionally, we found that many of our clergy were in desperate need of authentic connection and encouragement. It can be very lonely and unhealthy to pastor. Clergy who met monthly ended up doing wellness and accountability checks and also served as one another's backups during vacations and sometimes even sabbath days (see chapter 1). This strategy met the relational needs of clergy to connect with other colleagues.

- **Then, there must be a commitment to meaningful cluster goal setting (which requires relationship building among laity).**
  Meaningful cluster goal setting involves all five of Jesus's organizing principles (chapter 2) because one can't have a meaningful goal without a shared vision that includes the needs of the community outside the walls of the church.

- **Finally, there must be a commitment to aligning individual congregational goal setting toward this cluster goal.**
  This isn't about adding the cluster goal to the individual, congregational goal, but about describing how each goal builds on another toward the cluster goal. We didn't quite get to this within three years, but it is essential, if we are serious about creating an environment in which we are expecting all persons to pursue mission strategy. It takes courage to pursue something with a larger group of others for the sake of kingdom fruit that may or may not result in more people in worship or more money in the collection plate (or equivalent).

Maximizing Assets: Strategy, Leadership, and Buildings

In mainline denominations, there are huge opportunities to maximize leadership, social capital, and physical assets. Yet many judicatory leaders are spending the majority of their time on crises instead of on maximizing these three things. Let's explore what it looks like to maximize these three things at the judicatory or denominational level and then what shifts might need to be made in order to free up time to invest in these areas.

On Strategy

In a recent orientation for new district superintendents and directors of connectional ministries, we were challenged to intentionally shift our focus to a particular segment of churches so that resources of time, treasure, and talent were maximized. Lisa Greenwood from the Texas Methodist Foundation described the general trend something like this:

- Ten to twenty percent of your churches are vital. They typically don't demand a lot of conference time or resources. If they do ask for help, give it to them.

- Fifty-five to sixty-five percent of your churches are in the middle, but some are more or less ready to make a change. Invest your time in the part of the middle that is ready to make a change that leads them to be vital; invest less time in the churches that are not ready.

- Thirty to forty percent of your churches are dying. They typically demand a lot of attention as they have fiscal or physical plant crises. Investing time here is not wise; yet ask annual conference leaders and you will soon find out the majority of their time is spent here.

Appendix

Visually, the trends looked like this:

Vital Congregations: 15%

■■■■■■■■■■
■■■■■

Stagnant or Declining Congregations: 50%
Half: Ready

■■■■■■■■■■
■■■■■■■■■■
■■■■■

The Other Half: Not Ready

□□□□□□□□□□
□□□□□□□□□□
□□□□□

Dying Congregations: 35%

□□□□□□□□□□
□□□□□□□□□□
□□□□□

Predictably, people in the room asked: but what do we do with those churches that are in crisis and aren't getting resources of time, talent, and treasure? There were several ideas put forward for those who were in the bottom two categories ("stagnant" or "declining and not ready," and "dying"): asking retired pastors to serve as accompaniers, creating a team of conflict resolution specialists, and implementing a process for closing churches. These were somewhat unsurprising answers. Lisa's response was a bit unorthodox as she guided the group to think about the real cost of developing, implementing, and supporting these initiatives. We wouldn't want to detract from the real target: next-level congregations or those that are ready but not yet vital.

She challenged us to think about what it would really take to focus 80 percent of our time on the top two groups, with the majority of our time on the not-yet-vital-but-ready group. As we continued dialogue around this, it was clear that most annual conferences weren't structured to begin to think about this. And most leaders were troubled by the idea of focusing only on a subset of the faith communities within their midst.

Church leaders seem simultaneously profoundly uncomfortable with the notion of pronouncing the death of a congregation and surprised when a congregation that looks like it is dying actually turns around and becomes vital. I (Christie) think that is one reason why we have so many churches that are in the bottom category. Some leaders won't close a congregation because they believe everything can be turned around (but don't necessarily know how to position it to do that), and others won't close a congregation because they can't deal with the idea of it. However, we shouldn't focus just on church closures but on honest assessments of readiness and whether or not the gathered people of God have the will and the why lined up for forming and multiplying neighborhood-changing disciples. We are fighting a spiritual battle, and if the team we have on the front lines is no longer interested in fighting or not able to fight, we need to change the team.

We could say *yes* and *amen* to the model only if the process for sorting faith communities was transparent and honored congregational input and history. In order for judicatories to maximize assets, they must invest in using an assessment and planning process with integrity: readiness is not seen by numbers in worship, but by the degree to which the remnant is spiritually vibrant, healthy in their relationships, willing to make sacrifices necessary to focus on the mission, and open to people who are different than themselves. These are the hidden assets within faith communities that can only be known through honest inquiry. I have been surprised again and again when judicatory or denominational leaders mistake size of the worshipping community for vitality. Health—and the lack thereof—comes in all shapes, contexts, and sizes.

Appendix

The key to maximizing utilization in my (Joe's) opinion is making sure that our leadership, social capital, and physical assets are moving to the places and spaces where mission strategy matters the most: on the ground. Oftentimes, our strictures and structures within judicatories and local churches are not set up for this to happen. But when the setup is right, optimum results can be achieved.

A great illustration of this is the US Army's military theatre of operations. I remember accompanying a friend and colleague to a leadership conference out west. While traveling, we stopped to see my friend's brother, who at the time was a military officer. We began talking with him about realities and hopes and dreams in the church, and our conversation spurred him to take us to see the theatre of operations that the army uses every time they land in a place of war or battle.

I was enamored as my friend's brother showed and described the theatre. Everything in the theatre, he said, is focused on the front lines. The battle, the war, he said, is won on the front lines, and so every resource (asset) that comes into the theatre is positioned to go to the front lines. I asked him who was on the front lines. He said that the best soldiers that the army has to offer are on the front lines, and it is the responsibility of the generals and the other officers in the theatre to make sure that the systems and the operations of the theatre get the resources to the soldiers so that they can fight with optimum capacity. The generals are in the back of the theatre, in the place where the resources come in. Their sole task in the theatre is to get the resources to the front where the battle is won or lost.

When my friend's brother finished, I was aghast. Because what he had shown me was the opposite of how I saw most churches and judicatories. Most of the models I'd seen in the church, particularly in denominational offices, moved resources from the front lines to across the church, so that the denominational body was funded sometimes at the expense of those on the front lines. In the church, pastors and laypeople are on the front lines. And it is the responsibility of the local church, our ordaining councils, and, in the case of episcopal denominations, bishops and the like to deploy the best we have to the places where the wars really need to be won.

But oftentimes the assets move from the front lines to the back of the theatre where top leadership decides how resources are shared and deployed, rather than the other way around. I believe this is a major reason why the church loses too many wars in key places—in urban cities where gentrification is displacing the marginalized, in rural areas where unemployment and the opioid crisis are rearing their ugly heads, and in suburbs where the seduction of privilege has caused too many families and individuals to crumble due to the neglect of a hungry, malnourished soul.

What would it look like if denominational offices only had the necessary employees in it to strengthen and serve the front lines and if most of the denominational staff took on roles of leadership on the front lines in addition to their denominational work? What if bishops led a church in the most strategic missional location in the judicatory or denomination, but had the necessary staff in that church to be free to model mission strategy for all under her or his episcopal purview? What if there were more superintendents and the like pastoring churches in a smaller region, again having the necessary staff support to free them to do mission strategy with their colleagues in a smaller, targeted area? What if judicatories had a human resources department to handle all personnel, benefits, and conflict-management issues that arose? What if judicatories had finance departments responsible for disseminating resources to the front lines as well as managing properly the resources that come in to help the front lines? What if judicatories had a congregational and pastoral leadership development department to help equip those on the front lines? What if judicatories determined what shared ministries needed to be a part of it, and which ones could be disseminated, to maximize global, regional, and local mission? And what if everybody else was deployed into the field, using their assets to reach more disciples for Jesus Christ on the front lines, as well as to meet more tangible needs on the front lines?

Appendix

It seems to me that if this model were enacted, we would be in a better position to maximize our assets. We have to find new ways of ensuring the right leaders are in the right seats to support the advancement of the kingdom of God on the ground. When we maximize our leadership, social capital, and physical assets in these or other similar ways, the kingdom of God here on earth can be manifest and can reveal itself to a hungry and hurting world in a much more powerful, relevant manner.

There are some interesting differences and synergy between the approaches we shared:

1. The notion of letting vibrant churches help drive the decision-making, for example, is consistent in both. If a vital church says it needs help, give it! If a vital church says it sees a way to expand the kingdom, listen to it! If troops on the front line who have proven their ability to advance the mission need resources, give it! If they see a way to advance the mission that wasn't on the original plan, listen to it! It takes humble, selfless, collaborative leadership to make this work.

2. If we used the theatre-of-operations analogy, it works when the church on the front line is vital, but it wouldn't work for churches on the front line who are not vital. Going back to the military example, if a unit isn't vital it dies, and therefore that team of individuals doesn't continue to receive resourcing. If the position is a strategic one, generals may choose to send in a proven battalion or a special team to regain ground. Too often, if a church isn't vital there may be no other consequence than its struggle to keep the lights on. Some of our church buildings are no longer in a strategic position in their communities. Some teams are no longer able to fight the good fight of kingdom advancement. There are things to be learned from both of these.

3. The model of focusing 80 percent of our attention on a third of the faith communities could drive some healthy conversations

about vitality and readiness that are rooted in the holistic model of Jesus as opposed to statistics. We would have some concerns about how this model might get translated and implemented both in how faith communities would be categorized and in how they would be treated. It is essential that definitions of vitality include measures of transformational impact and not just counting money and people! It is essential that congregations participate in a meaningful way in the assessment, instead of it being a determination by jurisdictional leaders based upon their intuition, a statistical analysis, and implicit or explicit cultural biases. Some annual conferences ask churches to evaluate their vitality at each charge conference and then do a deeper dive with churches that don't match the judicatory leader's assessment for mutual learning.

4. Both approaches require the adoption of whole new mindsets, measurement tools, and staffing models. Because of that, it can be easy for some to dismiss either model out of hand for being unrealistic or impossible to implement in a given judicatory. However, we serve a God who makes all things possible and all things new. We realize that we both—in different ways—may have challenged something that you, the reader, hold dear. Examining and challenging assumptions is a healthy part of continuing to grow and evolve as leaders and institutions.

On Leadership

We need everyone in ministry—lay and clergy of all positions and in all places—to roll up their sleeves, get dirty, and seek to make a huge difference in the lives of hurting people in our communities, day in and day out. That cannot happen if we only sit in a comfortable office pushing papers and responding to calls and emails, whether or not we are judicatory or local church leaders. The work is in the local faith communities and the neighborhoods that surround them. I (Joe) am a huge proponent of bishops and superintendents pastoring churches simultaneously. Having served as district superintendent and pastor at the same time, I have seen firsthand the power of mission strategy that connects the institution and local church for change. So often, there is a disconnect between what is happening at the judicatorial level and what is happening on the ground.

One leads differently when one has to be accountable for the very things he or she is asking his or her colleagues to produce. It's one thing to sit in an office and demand apportionments; it's another thing to work within a congregation that has to justify them in the midst of many competing needs! It's one thing to sit in an office and expect worship attendance to rise; it's another thing to have to lead congregations in developing creative ways to reach more people for Jesus Christ!

We believe that there are many opportunities for collaborating while maintaining appropriate authority and roles that various leaders play. The appointment process in The United Methodist Church is one of those things that can help or hurt mission strategy. I (Joe) have offered the idea that pastors of vital congregations be allowed and approached to come alongside bishops and superintendents to assist with the appointment process. Who best knows a community than a vital church pastor and vital church leaders who live, breathe, and work there every day? These people can offer a great deal of information to the appointment process and help with building a neighborhood team that can collectively bring revitalization.

A bridge across this disconnect happens when we begin valuing those who have been doing mission strategy at the local church level and seek to creatively position them to lead beyond their local church. In too many cases, we have institutional leaders who do not understand mission strategy because they have not practiced it in the places where it truly makes a difference. Therefore, when they are promoted to judicatorial positions that demand this type of leadership, they are lost. Additionally, we risk harming local churches when we pull mission strategists out of local faith communities and into the institution. This is another argument to be made for adopting a dual role or a both-and solution. Building the bridge means positioning people with a track record who understand and who have successfully practiced mission strategy at the local level. This track record of doing mission strategy is essential. We need to value those who have mission strategy experience.

On Buildings

We need to learn how to repurpose property and need to have the courage to do so. We will often keep dying congregations of twenty-five people or less going, in buildings that are falling apart and cannot be maintained, for many reasons. Four of the most popular are: (1) we need a place to appoint pastors; (2) we need the relatively small apportionment check they are paying in order to support the judicatory budget; (3) we don't want to bother with the difficult decision and process of repurposing a church, when repurposing might just be the blessing that the local church, community, and judicatory really need; and (4) we don't want to be involved with closing a church and the painful reality that brings to people's and a community's lives. What if we got creative and innovative and partnered with these congregations to figure out ways to repurpose their property and revive their congregations in fresh, dynamic ways? It may call for some unpopular decisions in the short term, but in the long term, growth can happen.

Liberating Congregations: On Encouraging Experimentation

Judicatories must intentionally create space and actively encourage experimentation with new ways of being the church. In the Greater Washington District, we had two grand experiments underway: InspireDC and the 20019 zip code. InspireDC was a hub for developing ministry with and for young adults. And 20019 was a zip code in one of the economically poorest areas of the city. There are four United Methodist churches in this zip code and an opportunity to clarify a joint strategy so that community partnerships might be developed. We also created space in charge conferences for dreaming and goal setting within the cluster context. Each space afforded us a view of where leaders and congregations were on the continuum of liberation. Each space exposed the operating assumptions of leaders and congregations (e.g., Who gets to count the new people who come to worship or serve? Whose church is hosting? How often do we meet?)

Another thing that judicatories can do to create an environment of innovation is actively promoting new faith expressions with and for new people on micro and macro levels. For years, there has been a false dichotomy between revitalizing existing churches and planting new churches, between equipping pastors and equipping planters. We seem to have forgotten the natural order of things:

- growing and multiplying disciples (each one infected with Jesus DNA) before

- multiplying small groups (apprentice leadership within accountable community that grows and multiplies disciples) before

- multiplying missional communities or worship services (leadership teams that create community and plan regular experiences that grow and multiply disciples).

New faith expressions grow out of a context of a faith community that is doing at least the first two things, whether that "expression" is a new site of an existing church, a new venture that doesn't look like church, a new missional community, or a repurposing of an existing church building.

Angie Thurston and Casper ter Kuile have gained much recognition (and funding) for their work that started with mapping a host of new organizations that deepen community with millennials in ways that are powerful, surprising, and perhaps even religious. They have researched and published a total of five reports including their seminal work, "How We Gather."[1]

Recently they collaborated with the Texas Methodist Foundation for a report called "Faithful."[2] The report was designed especially for denominational leaders across traditions who are wrestling with the tension of improving existing congregational models versus creating fresh models of religious life with emerging leaders. As Sid Schwarz states,

> A faithful response is to shepherd emergence. To look not only at the edge of our tradition, but beyond it. To see a new generation of leaders—often the products of our own summer camps, youth programs, and congregations—and find ways to support their, and their communities', flourishing.[3]

There is tension between improving and creating that goes far beyond resistance to change. This point is raised by Gil Rendle in his essay "Waiting for God's New Thing: Spiritual and Organizational Leadership in the In-Between Time—or—Why Better Isn't Good Enough,"[4] and is reiterated in "Faithful":

> IMPROVING entails learning new ways to do what we already know how to do with and for people we already know how to relate to.
>
> CREATING requires learning new ways to do what we don't yet know how to do—and may be disallowed to do by existing polity and practice with and for those we don't know how to relate to.[5]

Improving is within the scope of established institutions, but *creating* is beyond it.

We believe that judicatories must create environments that support research and development and centralized so that resources can be directed to the best missional investment overall, and some should be localized because ministry and missional innovation are very contextual.

Leaders need to understand that benchmarks and strategic plans work when we are seeking to improve, but they are deadly and unhelpful for research and development. In our work with both the Texas Methodist Foundation and the Transformational Index, we have come to understand the difference in what measurements look like when we are seeking to improve something that is already working versus operating in an area that isn't working or where we don't know how. In the first instance we can learn from best practices; in the second instance there are no best practices (what other people have done in other contexts cannot simply be imported into your context). The key question is: are we building something new (including in the midst of a major organizational change effort) or improving something that is understood and exists and is working well? If the former, you are in design phase, and the impact measures are about progress, confidence, and learning; it is difficult to measure something that doesn't yet exist.

When a person or church has a vision of ministry that hasn't been pursued before, they are in design territory and need to be very intentional about testing and measuring. Design phase measures need to operate within the framework of a clear mission with indicators of impact (what does "good" look like?) identified, and they need to focus on the innovation itself.

A good measurement in the design phase is:

a. A leading (not lagging) indicator so that you get real time data for fast feedback. Caloric intake is a leading indicator, the pounds you weigh is a lagging indicator.

b. High touch and interaction (e.g., conversations with people instead of emailed surveys). You can read a demographic report, but cannot truly learn, design, and iterate without engaging the people you are reading about.

c. Focused on innovation, which means we experiment with evidence instead of trying to measure something we think might matter. (e.g.: To what extent do we see x? How confident are we that we are moving toward x?)

If you are seeking to do an online survey, in the initial round there should be no multiple choice—because you won't learn as much and you may miss an important choice option. Subsequent rounds could include testing statements gleaned from the first round and must include the option of "Other."

As you seek to measure progress in the design phase, consider asking one or more of the following:

a. To what extent do you feel we have made progress toward our stated purpose?

b. To what extent are we moving toward a shared purpose?

c. How confident are we that we are making progress toward this indicator or mission? What evidence do we have that we are making progress?

d. What was the most useful (highest value) of _____?

e. What are we learning?

f. How well equipped do you feel to experiment and learn by the evidence?[6]

> **"What if, instead of spending our time trying to keep all our current congregations working, we spent energy growing fresh expressions of faith?"**
>
> —Rev. Alex Shanks
> Assistant to Bishop Ken Carter,
> Florida Annual Conference (UMC)

What if we actually sought to create an environment and expectation of innovation for lay and clergy? What if we started to help people and faith communities articulate and measure impact in a way that encouraged a cycle of testing, learning, and pivoting as needed? What if we encouraged a new economic imagination that wasn't linked to the offering plate or denominational resources but resourced leaders to develop and test plans and pitches so that the invisible capitol around them was mobilized?

These are tips from our collective experiences in seeking to connect for a change. We have found that when we seek to be creative and innovative around some of these ideas, we are in a better position to engage people, churches, and partners in inspiring hope with their communities. We hope that the church and, in particular, church leaders will have the courage to stretch ourselves to be the change agents Jesus has called us to be!

Notes

Introduction

1. Bob Farr, Doug Anderson, and Kay Kotan, *Get Their Name: Grow Your Church by Building New Relationships* (Nashville: Abingdon Press, 2013).

1. Build Relationships

1. Jay Pathak, Dave Runyon, *The Art of Neighboring: Building Genuine Relationships Right Outside Your Door* (Ada, MI: Baker Books, 2012).

2. Junius Dotson at Discipleship Ministries has amplified this concept through the #SeeAllthePeople campaign and resources. See https://www.seeallthepeople.org/.

3. Mark 10:46-52.

2. Organize People

1. Joseph W. Daniels Jr., *Walking with Nehemiah: Your Community Is Your Congregation* (Nashville: Abingdon Press, 2014).

2. As quoted in Stedman Graham's *Diversity: Leaders Not Labels* (New York: Free Press, 2006).

3. From King's address at the Freedom Rally in Cobo Hall, Detroit, Michigan in 1963; published in *A Call to Conscience: The Landmark Speeches of Dr. Martin Luther King, Jr.* by Clayborne Carson and Kris Shepard (New York: Warner Books, 2001).

4. Karl Barth is associated with the quote, and also actress Dorothy

Bernhard, however it is originally from the short poem, "Courage," by Karle Wilson Baker, published in *Poetry*, October 1921.

3. Utilize Assets

1. See https://www.umcdiscipleship.org/resources/romans-12-project-overview.

2. Wayne Cordeiro in *The Divine Mentor: Growing Your Faith as You Sit at the Feet of the Savior* (Bloomington, MN: Bethany House Publishers, 2007).

3. See https://www.undergroundnetwork.org/who-we-are-index/.

4. Liberate Congregations

1. George Bullard Jr. used ten stages to describe the life cycle of a church, including birth, infancy, childhood, adolescence, adulthood, maturity, empty nest, retirement, old age, and death. See George Bullard's Journey blog and ebooks, "Captured by Vision" published by The Columbia Partnership, ColumbiaMetro, at www.bullardjournal.org. Our colleague, Andy Lunt, has simplified Ballard's image to focus on three main church diagnostic cycles: growth, stability, and decline—as expressed in the diagram. Diagram adapted from swmnelca.org/2013/04/03/congregation-planning-tool, accessed 13 February 2019.

2. Howard Thurman, *Jesus and the Disinherited* (Boston: Beacon Press, 2012).

3. Gary Keller and Jay Papasan, *The ONE Thing: The Surprisingly Simple Truth behind Extraordinary Results* (Austin, TX: Bard Press, 2013), https://www.the1thing.com/.

4. Charles F. Stanley, "11 Special Attributes of the Holy Spirit: Our Source of Power" at InTouch Ministries blog, August 15, 2018. See https://www.intouch.org/Read/Blog/11-special-attributes-of-the-holy-spirit.

Appendix

1. "How We Gather" is a reporting effort of a millennial-led

spiritual startup collaboration between Harvard Divinity School, the Fetzer Institute, and *On Being*. Learn more about Angie Thurston and Casper ter Kuile's work at www.howwegather.org/reports.

2. "Faithful" is a report written for denominational leaders across traditions developed by Harvard Divinity School Innovation fellows Casper ter Huile and Angie Thurston, in collaboration with colleagues Sue Phillips, Lisa Greenwood, and Gil Rendle. The content shares ideas from senior leaders in Jewish, Christian, and Unitarian Universalist communities. "Faithful" and other reports are available at www.howwegather.org/reports.

3. Sid Schwarz, *Finding a Spiritual Home: How a New Generation of Jews Can Transform the American Synagogue* (Woodstock, VT: Jewish Lights Publishing, 2003).

4. Gil Rendle, "Waiting for God's New Thing: Spiritual and Organizational Leadership in the In-Between Time–or–Why Better Isn't Good Enough" published by Texas Methodist University in Austin, Texas. April 2015. Non-altered reproduction and distribution with appropriate attribution is encouraged and authorized.

5. From "Faithful." See www.howwegather.org/reports.

6. From notes taken during mentoring conversations with Andy Schofield and Mark Sampson from the Transformational Index Group. "The TI is a tool that helps organizations quickly identify their intended social impact and measure progress in a way which balances a commitment to values with a focus on results." See http://www.thetransformationalindex.org.

www.ingramcontent.com/pod-product-compliance
Lightning Source LLC
Chambersburg PA
CBHW062116080426
42734CB00012B/2882